Professional Business Etiquette & Grooming

A Survival Skill to give You a Competitive Edge!

Gerard Assey

Professional
Business Etiquette
& Grooming

By
Gerard Assey
© Copyright 2022 by Author

Published by:
Gerard Assey
19/18, Palli Arasan Street
Anna Nagar East
Chennai - 600 102

ISBN: 978-81-952564-2-6

Cover Image: Image by rawpixel.com on Freepik- Courtesy www.Freepik.com
Due acknowledgement is provided. Thank you.

Table of Contents

Etiquette-A Survival Skill
to give you a Competitive Edge!

What is 'Etiquette'?- noun - 'et·i·quette'
It is the standard, a set of rules or customs that control accepted behavior in particular social groups or social situations- the courteous conduct in society and among individuals.
In today's increasingly global arena, technical knowledge alone is not enough to ensure success. Sophistication is more and more the catchword. Given a choice between two equally talented individuals, corporations will choose the candidate with greater interpersonal and social grace skills to represent it. As our world becomes a smaller place and our economy becomes increasingly global in scope, it is becoming increasingly clear how important good manners are in all cultures. In fact knowing how to treat others well is more important now than ever. By examining how good manners apply to our working world, we will benefit ourselves, together with everyone around us. After all who we are shows in how we behave and how we appear to others. How we look, talk, walk, sit, stand, eat. ie; how we present ourselves-speaks volumes about who we are and creates the first impression that others form of us. This is true not only in personal life but more so in our professional life. With a world that's becoming more and more competitive, proper business etiquette and interpersonal skills play an increasingly important role in the success or failure of anyone's business career and the company they represent. Knowing how to behave courteously and

professionally is far from trivial. Etiquette and protocol do count in the business world, as no matter how brilliant an employee may be, his or her lack of social grace can make a bad first impression on clients and business associates.

Take a look at the following.

Less than 30% of U.S. (the world's largest economy) businesspersons sent abroad can be expected to succeed. Training for employees prior to an overseas assignment can save companies tens of thousands of dollars, benefit the employee, and increase the company's chances of being successful… The Wall Street Journal

The Japanese (the world's second largest economy) *spend an estimated $900 million a year on training, related to etiquette and protocol*… Diana Rowland, California Japanese business practices consultant.

The importance of etiquette is thousands of years old. Around 2500B.C. the first etiquette manuscript gave this advice to young Egyptian men on the fast track: "*When sitting with one's superior, laugh when he laughs.*" The Instructions of Ptahhotep.

John Rockefeller once said: '*I will pay more for the ability to get along with people than for any other ability*'.

40 percent of all adults have social anxiety, and 75 percent of all adults experience anxiety at a party with strangers (from: Dr Bella De Paulo's: People Often Can't Judge How They Impress Others).

The World's Top Consultant, Peter Drucker was quoted as saying, "*Be ready or be lost; if you don't think globally you deserve to be unemployed and you will be.*"- Business Week.

You cannot imagine how necessary it is to mind all these little things; for I have seen many people with great talents ill received - Lord Chesterfield.

Studies have shown that more than 60% of what is believed about us is based upon visual messages-What people see!
At many Fortune 500 companies, top management take potential front line employees to lunch or dinner to observe their comfort level with executives, spouses, waiters and even with the various pieces of silverware. Like it or not, management equates good manners with competence and poor manners with incompetence. Table manners can make or mar a mega-merger, especially in an era when companies are competing on the basis of service-this can be a crucial business skill. Good manners are good business!
Your inability to handle yourself as is expected could be expensive--no one will tell you the real reason you didn't get the job, the promotion, that big business deal or the social engagement. Your social graces and general demeanor can tell as much about you as the way you handle an issue. Fair or not, others equate bad manners with incompetence and a lack of breeding, and the cumulative effect of this repeated faux pas in an organization, can be devastating leading to a major loss of respect, credibility, loss of reputation, and business!
Your Success can start today with 'Professional Business Etiquette & Grooming'

This book will help increase your confidence in your image, business etiquette and interpersonal skills to help you build rapport and trust with your business customers and associates. Proper business and social etiquette will give you a competitive edge in today's market...in fact, it's the only survival skill required!

Being comfortable in a variety of environments and cultures is one of the end results of etiquette training and as the business world becomes increasingly diverse, there has been a tremendous awakening and realization that etiquette training increases Teamwork, Productivity, and Employee Retention resulting in Business Growth by helping everyone get along, and outclassing the Competition.

So go ahead and enjoy the rest of the book!

Part 1
Etiquette and Grooming Skills

Managing You-Positive First Impressions!

Have you ever wondered about the impressions you could create even before you open our mouth?

In a study carried out that I am about to share with you now, you will notice that people place more emphasis on what they SEE rather than on what they HEAR. So this only tells us that we need to be very careful with our body language and what we are projecting.

According to studies carried out, Communication takes place in 3 forms:
- ✓ Your Words
- ✓ Your Tone and
- ✓ Your Body Language.

Where 55% has to do with your Body Language or what others 'See'

7 % has to do with 'What' you say or your words

Whilst 38% has to do with 'How' those words are said, which is your Tone or voice modulation

With people going by what they SEE first rather than what they HEAR, it makes it very important for us to therefore project the RIGHT image upfront. That's the first impression that has been formed-good or bad! If it is good, then very good for you, but if it is bad, then so sad! Because…now you have double work to undo the wrong impression that has already gone into the mind and to now fill it with the right impression.

They say 90% of lasting impressions are created in the first 90 seconds. That can be really dangerous, but surprisingly that is true! So we have to be very careful, with what are we projecting as soon as someone sees us, because that's what they will remember.

It is also a reason why we tend to remember a song seen on a television set better than when heard through a radio. The same logic applies at a job interview with your resume and the presentation of it! Then at the interview-the interviewer has made up his mind to a great extent as you walk in, even before you have opened your mouth. Your bio-profile or the interview process is only a confirmation of the decision already made in the mind of the interviewer.

Why is Tone next important after Body Language? Simply because you can say a same sentence with a different tone and that can change the entire meaning

Eg; "Mary come here" is a simple sentence. But depending on the right tone, this one sentence could turn out as an 'order 'or a 'request'.

Another stronger example: "Hang him not let him go"…could be death or life depending on how it is said. Example: 'Hang him, not let him go'! Or 'Hang him not, let him go'!

Now, if it is face to face, we may be able to save the situation, but when on the phone with the other person not able to see you, it could lead to miscommunication if the right tone is not used.

As seen earlier, with people going by what they 'See' first rather than what they 'Hear', it makes it so very important for us to therefore project the RIGHT image upfront. It basically involves Selling Yourself first!

Before a customer buys anything or decides to do business with you or the company that you represent, he needs to first be sold on you because you are what he sees about your company to him.

Your company could have a several floor building, with several offices all across the globe. But to the person doing business with you, what he sees in you is the impression he has formed of your company! Because…90% of lasting impressions are created in the first 90 seconds

A person forms an impression of you, usually in less than ten seconds, based on a combination of some of these attributes:

Posture, Walk
Body language
Attire, Clothing
Physical characteristics
Smile, Facial features
Handshake
Cleanliness, Grooming
Scent, perfume
Eye contact
Perceived Confidence

In a study, men and women were asked to list the attributes they found attractive and unattractive in someone they met. And here is the list of some of the top responses:

Qualities that create a Positive Impression:
- ✓ Warmth
- ✓ Sense of humor
- ✓ Imagination
- ✓ Fitness
- ✓ Individuality
- ✓ Positive body language
- ✓ Conversational ability
- ✓ Creativity
- ✓ Kindness

Qualities that create a Negative Impression
- ✓ Self-centered
- ✓ Closed minded
- ✓ Judgmental
- ✓ Lack of manners
- ✓ Poor conversational ability
- ✓ Negative attitude
- ✓ Indecisiveness
- ✓ Lack of integrity
- ✓ Complaining and whining
- ✓ Politics and Power games
- ✓ Manipulation

Making a Great First Impression

If you want to make a good impression, know that you need to project **3 C's:**
- ✓ Confidence
- • Have a straight but relaxed posture. Hold your head high and steady. Don't slouch or slump.
- • Move in a natural, unaffected manner.
- • Maintain eye contact with the people you are talking to.
- ✓ Competence
- • Exhibit your knowledge when required. Know your way around the agenda. Be prepared for the meeting. Bring supportive materials to emphasize your points.
- • Answer questions in a clear and professional manner, avoiding the use of slang or technical jargon.
- • Ask relevant questions if needed.
- ✓ Credibility
- • Arrive on time.
- • Be presentable (well-groomed and mindful of dress codes)

- Keep true to your word.
- When uncertain, err on the side of what you presume is conservatism. And be observant; check if people are becoming uncomfortable.
- Etiquette mishaps can range from merely embarrassing to potentially insulting to the other person. When you realize that you have committed a faux pas, apologize immediately and ask how you can make up for it

Appearance IS Everything! It starts with your Personal Grooming

Paying attention to your grooming by taking care of your cleanliness and your clothing demonstrates respect for yourself and for others- the key words being neat and clean.

- ✓ A general rule of thumb is: the more expensive the products/services you sell, the more professional you should look-Customers make assumptions about you based on your appearance.
- ✓ If it's an expensive product you are selling, the customer is bound to think: "How can this person help us make this expensive purchase when he can't even afford a proper wardrobe and take care of himself?"

Projecting the Right Image!

- ✓ How you dress, how you groom yourself and how you handle yourself in public is all part of your "packaging"
- ✓ Like product packaging, you can present yourself to be most appealing. And, you can present yourself differently according to the time and place.

✓ Presence is how you "present" yourself- it's your self-confidence, poise and appeal.

So what does it take to make a Special, Positive, and Instant Impression when prospective 'buyers' first see you.

According to Drew Westen, in his fabulous book "The Political Brain" one of the main determinants of electoral success," he explains, "is simply a candidate's curb appeal". Curb appeal is the feeling voters get when they 'drive by' a candidate a few times on television and form an emotional impression! Personal Curb Appeal is primarily a nonverbal process.

How's your Personal Curb Appeal? When your co-workers, clients, and business partners "drive by" you, how do you come across? Here are a few tips to keep in mind:

- ✓ Dress for success: Always dress and see yourself for the next level!
- ✓ Your motto should be: "Wear great clothes. You never know whom you'll meet!" When it comes to curb appeal, the way you dress matters. Clothing has an effect on both the observer and the wearer.
- ✓ Dressing for success doesn't necessarily mean you have to wear a suit to work. Many organizations have a more casual dress code. But it does mean that whatever you wear should help you make the statement that you are a competent professional.

The finest clothing made is a person's skin, but, of course, society demands something more than this- Mark Twain

Wardrobe Management

Your dress is either working for you or against you. Clothes send a message about how you want others to see you. The way you dress can play a big role in your professional career. Part of the culture of a company is the dress code of its employees. Some companies prefer a business casual approach, while other companies require a business professional dress code.

These guidelines provided, are only suggestions, as you would need to always research the event, function, occasion or environment in question to determine the appropriate dress attire. Each industry-professional, community, and academic, may sometimes follow its own wardrobe standards and traditions.

But remember: If you are not too sure when business casual is appropriate, then always remember the general rule of thumb: *It's better to be over-dressed, than under-dressed.*

Professional Dressing:

Business attire suggests formal, conservative dress style. Attention to detail, impeccable grooming, and a well-fitting suit are vital to make a good lasting impression.

The Suit: Choose a classic, neutral suit in charcoal, black, grey or navy. Avoid suits that conform to trends. Best fabrics for suits are wool/wool blends which can be worn all year and do not wrinkle easily. Skirt suits are appropriate feminine attire as long as the skirt hits or covers the knee and there are no large slits at the side, front, or back. The pant leg should touch the front of the shoe and fall just above the heel in the back. Make sure the suit flatters your body type and fits well, not too tight or loose.

The Dress Shirt: Choose shirts in a pale, subtle color (i.e., blue, cream, white, baby pink). Long sleeved, button-up shirts are most appropriate. Your shirt sleeve should extend beyond the suit jacket sleeves by half an inch. Pointed collars give a more professional image than button-down collars, yet both are acceptable. Choose shirts with more cotton than polyester; they resist wrinkling.

Shoes/Socks/Belt/Accessories etc:

Shoes: Leather in lace-ups shoes and should not be lighter than the trouser color. Shoes that match your suit or are slightly darker are the best choice in colors, such as brown, black, tan, or navy. The shoe should have a real sole (no sneakers, sandals, or street shoes) and a closed toe. Avoid platforms and heels higher than 2 inches. Shoes should be polished and in good condition. Wear black shoes with grey, navy or black suits and dark brown shoes with tan, brown or beige suits.

Socks: Preferable 100% cotton in black, brown, grey or navy. Choose a color to match or blend with trousers. Be sure to wear socks that cover your calves.

Ties: Tie and suit color should complement each other, but not match. Burgundy, red and navy blue work as good background colors. Small geometric prints and stripes are good choices. Paisleys with subdued patterns are alternatives. Silk ties are the preferred choice. They are elegant and can be worn all year in any climate. The tie knot should fill the space at the top of the shirt. Do not wear a matching handkerchief/ pocket square.

Belts: Either leather or reptile in black, brown or burgundy. Use discreet brass or good metal buckles. Suspenders are acceptable. Belts should be in good condition and match the color of your shoes, avoiding fancy and flashy buckles.

Briefcases: Briefcase should ideally be brown, black or burgundy leather, matching your shoes

Accessories: Jewellery ideally should be no more than one ring per hand. Good quality watches. No earring or studs for men

The right business attire never includes the following:
- ✓ Jeans (of any color)
- ✓ Athletic wear (e.g. sweat suits)
- ✓ Leggings
- ✓ T-shirts
- ✓ Low-cut garments, front or back
- ✓ Any kind of workout clothes, running or gym shoes, sneakers or sandals
- ✓ Hats, caps
- ✓ Ripped or tattered clothing
- ✓ Extremely tight-fitting clothes

What to keep in mind when buying your garments?

Before making a purchase, men and women need to answer "yes" to these key questions. If you are in doubt, don't buy the item, as clothes should look and feel good.
- ✓ Did you try the garment on?
- ✓ Did you check the fit in the front and the back?
- ✓ Is the suit jacket long enough to cover the buttocks?
- ✓ Are the button holes sewn tightly?

- ✓ Can you move around freely in the garment?
- ✓ Does the product feel comfortable?
- ✓ Check for pulls, bulges or bunching of the material.
- ✓ Do you like the garment? Buy a garment because you like it, not just to add to your wardrobe

How to Wear a Blazer or Suit

When planning to wear a blazer or a suit, here are a few tips on using them the right way. The first thing that you might want to consider when wearing a men's suit is how many buttons it will have. Although this may seem insignificant, the truth is that it is very important.

- ✓ When you wear a 3-button suit, you will button the top or top two buttons.
- ✓ When you wear a 2-button suit, you will button only the top button.
- ✓ With a 4-button suit, it is typically acceptable to button the two middle buttons, leaving the top button and the bottom button undone
- ✓ With a double-breasted suit, all buttons are buttoned.

When wearing a suit or Blazer:

- ✓ If you are seated, your suit coat should always be open. It is not acceptable to take off your suit coat unless you are to be seated for an extended period of time, like for a meal, or in your office, or if your host does so, etc.
- ✓ If you wish to take your suit coat off in company, it is polite to ask permission (Eg; - Do you mind if I take my coat off?)
- ✓ You should always hang your suit coat, even if only over the back of your chair

Wearing a Necktie- Combinations, Knots and Care

A tie is a man's way to express his personality and style.

Before you put on your tie:

- ✓ Check to make sure that the tie is clean, without any stains, grease or food spots
- ✓ Cut any loose threads on your tie. Pulling them can do damage to your tie.
- ✓ When wearing a shirt, tie and jacket, stick to a maximum of two different patterns unless you have a very solid fashion sense and know how to mix and match clothing well. Your tie should ideally be darker than the color of your shirt
- ✓ Always tie the knot in front of a mirror.
- ✓ Ensure your shirt is buttoned up, with a tie collar and have the collar up before putting the tie around your neck.
- ✓ Keep the knot of the tie tight throughout the entire tying process.
- ✓ The front of your tie should be just long enough so that the tip touches the waist of your pants.
- ✓ The general width of a tie that will not get out of style of fashion is 3.5 inches.
- ✓ Ideally, the width of a tie should match the width of the jacket's lapel. If the jacket has a wide lapel, then the tie should be wide, and if narrow, then the tie is narrow.
- ✓ So also, the knot of the tie should be proportional to the collar. It should not be so big that it spreads the collar of the shirt or forces it open, or so small that it gets lost in the collar of the shirt.

Caring for your Ties:
- ✓ A tie that is properly cared for can last forever.
- ✓ Untie your tie completely and hang up your ties. It helps take out some of the wrinkles and prevents damage.
- ✓ Knit ties can be stretched when hung, so gently roll them up and store them in a drawer.
- ✓ Ideally, ties must be hung on a rack designed for ties. Ties slip and twist on hangers and will probably fall off.
- ✓ When traveling, loosely roll ties and place them inside a pair of socks or use a tie case or box.
- ✓ Don't wear the same tie twice in a row. Ties need time to return to their normal shape

How to Tie Necktie Knots

The Four in Hand Tie Knot (Probably the simplest way to tie a neck tie)

1. Start with the wide end on your right. Extend it about 30cm (ruler length) below the narrow end of your necktie
2. Cross the wide end over the narrow, and back underneath
3. Bring the wide end around passing it across the front of the narrow
4. Pass the wide end up through the loop
5. Hold the knot loosely and pass the wide end down through the loop in front.
6. Hold the narrow end of the tie and slide the knot up snug.

The Half Windsor Knot (Medium symmetrical triangle knot

1. Start with the wide end on your right. Extend it about 30cm (ruler length) below the narrow end of your necktie.

Necktie Knots

2. Cross the wide end over the narrow, and turn back underneath.
3. Bring the wide end up....
4. And turn down through loop.
5. Pass the wide end around the front from your left to right.
6. Then up through the loop
7. And then down through the knot in front
8. Tighten carefully and draw up to collar.

The Windsor Knot (Wide and triangular knot)
1. Start with the wide end on your right. Extend it about 30cm (ruler length) below the narrow end of your necktie.
2. Cross the wide end over the narrow, and bring up through the loop
3. Bring the wide end down, around behind the narrow end and up on your right
4. Pass the wide end around the front from your left to right
5. Then up through the loop
6. And then down through the knot in front.
7. Tighten carefully and draw up to collar

The meaning of colors in business that can help:
The colors you wear in professional settings and interviews can affect your mood, energy, and how others may perceive you. So you would want to wear colors that portray positive perceptions and exude confidence, sincerity, and reliability.
Here are some colors with their perceived meanings:
- ✓ Red: Action, powerful, passion and energetic
- ✓ Green: Growth, ideas, vitality and sophistication
- ✓ Blue: Inspires confidence, success and trust. Navy blue is best color for work/interviews – more likely to help create a positive vibe.
- ✓ Gold: Wealth, prosperity, luxury
- ✓ Black: Black looks classic and sophisticated, but perceived as depressing, serious or intimidating – so add a little color to black suits.
- ✓ Pink: Compassion, understanding and warmth. Pink or salmon worn by men is seen as a communicator color.

- ✓ Brown: Practical and reliable; sometimes perceived as dull
- ✓ Purple: Inventive, creative, intuitive. Dark purple can be perceived as elegant and projects authority.
- ✓ White: Clean, pure, innocent, and simple

Professional Business Attire

Men: A man's business suit is a standard item for business professional attire. Remember that your clothes should not attract more attention than the work you are doing

Ladies: Women have the versatility of choosing either a pair of dress slacks, or a skirt, with a business suit jacket. A matching pantsuit, skirt suit or even a professional dress and blazer can work. As long as your slacks are formal dress pants and look nice, they are acceptable. If you choose a skirt, it should have a comfortable fit that looks nice without being too-revealing. It's always safe to choose a skirt that hits the knee. When choosing a skirt, make sure that you can sit comfortably in public. Mini-skirts, for example, or skirts that are short and tight are inappropriate.

Informal-type pants such as jeans, sweat pants, leggings, spandex, or shorts should be avoided.

Professional Footwear: Conservative walking shoes, dress shoes, oxfords, loafers, boots, flats, dress heels, and backless shoes are acceptable for work. Not wearing stockings or socks is inappropriate.

Athletic shoes, tennis shoes, flip-flops, slippers, and any casual shoe with an open toe are not acceptable business formal footwear

Professional Accessories and Jewelry: Tasteful, professional ties, pocket squares, scarves, belts, and

jewelry are encouraged. Jewelry should be worn in good taste, with limited visible body piercings
Professional Makeup and Fragrances: A professional appearance is encouraged and excessive makeup is unprofessional. Remember that some people are allergic to the chemicals in perfumes and makeup, so wear these substances with restraint

Business Casual Attire

Men: A dress shirt and tie still looks nice, for example, but a full suit isn't necessary in a business casual environment. A nice dress shirt can be worn without a tie, yet still looks professional and put together. Dress pants in a lighter color can also be another option for a casual environment. A conservative leather belt adds a nice finish to this basic business casual outfit for men.

Ladies: Tops such as button-downs, sweaters, turtle necks, and blouses, for example, are suitable for the office. A fitted suit jacket paired with a blouse is appropriate for a business casual workplace

Business Casual Footwear: Conservative athletic or walking shoes, loafers, sneakers, boots, flats, dress heels, and leather deck-type shoes are acceptable. Wearing no stockings is acceptable in warm weather. Flashy athletic shoes, flip-flops, slippers, and any shoe with open toes are not acceptable in the office.

Business Casual Accessories and Jewelry: Accessories and jewelry should be worn in good taste, with limited visible body piercings

Business Casual Makeup and Fragrances: All products should be worn in good taste. Remember that some people are allergic to the chemicals in perfumes and makeup, so wear these substances with restraint.

Casual Attire

Casual Dressing: This is for casual Fridays or casual events. In general, this means clothes that are nice, but not dressy. This look can include jeans and khaki-type pants. Jeans should be dark wash and have no holes or extreme fading. Chinos or "Dockers"- type trousers, Polo shirts (with collars), Sweater or sport jackets are fine

Grooming Checklist

What could you do to improve your image- starting right from the top of your head to the tip of your toes- your hygiene, dressing and grooming, being organized etc.

Given below is a suggested checklist to help you project the Right Image!

Physical Aspects like:

- ✓ Personal Grooming-Dress for the next level!
- ✓ Cleanliness, Breath (floss/ use mouthwash), Hair well groomed, Nails, Body Odour (light deodorant)
- ✓ Clean, Wrinkle-free and Well-Pressed/ Proper fit clothes
- ✓ Check for stains/ lint/ holes/ loose buttons
- ✓ Pleasant Colours of Clothing
- ✓ Polished shoes and in good condition (don't let heels run down)
- ✓ Socks (clean without holes, foot deodorant?)
- ✓ Clean Spectacles
- ✓ Briefcase/ handbag well polished/ in good condition
- ✓ Business Cards in pristine, crisp condition (in a holder)
- ✓ Good quality pens that write!

- ✓ Standing- shoulder square/ sitting- erect
- ✓ Good Leather Bag/ Briefcase-organized /in order/ tidy

You might like to develop your own checklist now to suit your specific country and need.

(You might like to add on to the list above)

Body Language

As we've seen, people form 90% of their opinion of us in the first 90 seconds, a good example of just how powerful first impressions are! Being dressed for success is good but not enough in the competitive times in which we live. How many people do you know that impress us with their clothes but fail to impress us in other ways? Body language is the way you stand, sit, the way you move, and the way you present yourself. A major percentage of what we communicate has nothing to do with words.

We communicate in a lot of other ways-by the way we sit, stand, tense our facial muscles, tap our fingers, shuffle our feet and uncross or cross our legs. Without saying a word, our body language is broadcasting so many things about us!

So here are some quick tips on what to do and not do!

How to Look Interested

- ✓ Make strong eye contact
- ✓ Tilt your head slightly
- ✓ Don't fidget
- ✓ Look upward
- ✓ Lean forward slightly, weight on balls of feet.

When someone is friendly, we also think of him as trustworthy, sincere and reliable.

How to Stand the Right Way
- ✓ Stand squarely in front of the person to whom you are speaking.
- ✓ It might sound strange, but you expose your heart and body.
- ✓ Don't turn sideways.
- ✓ Meet their eyes in a friendly but steady gaze.
- ✓ Smile in a warm, relaxed way
- ✓ Don't hold a book or purse in front of you or cross your arms.
- ✓ Use open hand gestures.

Maintaining the Right Physical Distance
- ✓ If you watch a crowd, you will notice that people stand at different distances from each other.
- ✓ Less than 18 inches: intimate
- ✓ 18 inches- 2.5 feet: close friends in a social gathering. You can hold out your arm and you can stick your thumb in the other person's ear! Try it!
- ✓ 2.5-4 feet: most people in a casual setting
- ✓ 4-12 feet: strangers
- ✓ 12 feet: a group of strangers
- ✓ If you get too close, the other person will grow tense or withdraw

Making Eye Contact
- ✓ The eyes have it. Well, they truly do, and can project confidence when there are no words.
- ✓ To be a good listener, let your eyes convey: "I'm listening"

Here are some Signs that can indicate Nervousness. Try to work on controlling these:
- ✓ Eyes darting back and forth
- ✓ Tensing of the body
- ✓ Contraction of the body

- ✓ Shifting one's weight from side to side
- ✓ Rocking in chair
- ✓ Crossing and uncrossing the arms or legs
- ✓ Tapping hands, fingers, or feet
- ✓ Adjusting or fiddling with pens, cups, eyeglasses, jewelry, clothing, fingernails, hair, or hands wringing hands
- ✓ Clearing the throat
- ✓ Coughing nervously
- ✓ Smiling nervously
- ✓ Biting the lip
- ✓ Looking down
- ✓ Chewing nails or picking cuticles
- ✓ Putting hands in pockets

And here are some Signs that can indicate Boredom. Try and work on controlling these too:

- ✓ Moving your body frequently
- ✓ Letting your eyes wander
- ✓ Gazing into the distance
- ✓ Glancing often at your watch
- ✓ Yawning
- ✓ Tapping fingers or feet
- ✓ Fidgeting
- ✓ Picking your fingers or nails
- ✓ Avoiding eye contact

Sitting, Standing and Walking the Right Way

The Right Way to Sit- for a Lady: If you are in someone's home or at a big social event, never sit, till you are given permission to do so. The hostess may have planned on a particular place she would like you to sit. If no one offers you, then only take the seat of your choice. Walk towards the chair with good posture. Turn and feel the chair with the back of your knees, just to make sure that no one has "accidentally" moved the chair away. Sit down, keeping your back straight and your head up, while keeping your knees together and you hands in your lap. Cross your legs at the ankle or hold your feet together. In any event, make sure your knees are together

The Right Way to Sit- for a Gentleman: Walk to the chair with good posture, and as you approach the chair, unbutton your jacket. Sit tall with your back against the chair and knees slightly apart and both feet on the floor, with your hands resting just above your knees. When you stand up, remember to re-button your jacket

Standing: When you get up, keep your feet parallel but your knees relaxed. Ensure that your spine is long and straight, with your shoulders back, stomach in, chest high, chin turned up slightly and your arms and hands relaxed.

Walking: Stand as mentioned above and step with feet slightly ahead of your body. This promotes good posture

Other Points: Never lean on anything, as it denotes a careless attitude with 99% of your "presence" being lost when you lean.

Never greet someone with a handshake across the table (the only exception of course is when you're meeting someone and both of you are seated).

Always stand up when you are shaking hands. Greeting someone from behind a desk creates an instant barrier. Instead, always greet someone as your equal

Meeting and Greeting

Greeting someone you know is a vital part of courtesy and goodwill. All societies and cultures have some form of greeting that is basic to civilized interaction. The first point about greetings is to do them. It's important to say "hello" even when you feel a bit off or shy. It's also important to make introductions even when you're not certain of precisely how it should be done in that situation. Every greeting and introduction is an opportunity to demonstrate respect for others and to create a favorable impression of you to others.

Your goal therefore within the first few minutes of meeting and greeting other people is to make them feel comfortable and to put them at ease so they will want to do business with you. Doing so will make the first encounter and subsequent ones go smoothly and easily. Getting off on the wrong foot can cause a difficult recovery

So let's first start with the most important thing you could do when meeting someone that doesn't cost you anything, before we get into the etiquette of handshaking and business cards and the other areas: And that's your Smile!

Your Smile will take you a Mile! It's been said many times- smile when someone enters your office and do it with feeling. Nothing makes a client feel more welcomed than a warm and friendly smile. Check yourself in a mirror to see yourself as the customer might see you…SMILE!

A smile is an invitation, a sign of welcome. It says, "I'm friendly and approachable."

The human brain prefers happy faces, recognizing them more quickly than those with negative expressions. In fact, a smile is such an important signal to social interaction, that it can be recognized from 300 feet- more than a football field away.

Most importantly, smiling directly influences how other people respond to you. When you smile at someone, they almost always smile in return. And, because facial expressions trigger corresponding feelings, the smile you get back changes people's emotional state in a positive way. This one simple act will instantly and powerfully increase your curb appeal.

On the phone-Your customer will not hear it, but will see and feel it! It's such an important aspect that can say a lot about you! Remember, it's the first impression that will often be the one that they take away with them.

Handshakes and Business Card Etiquette
Handshakes

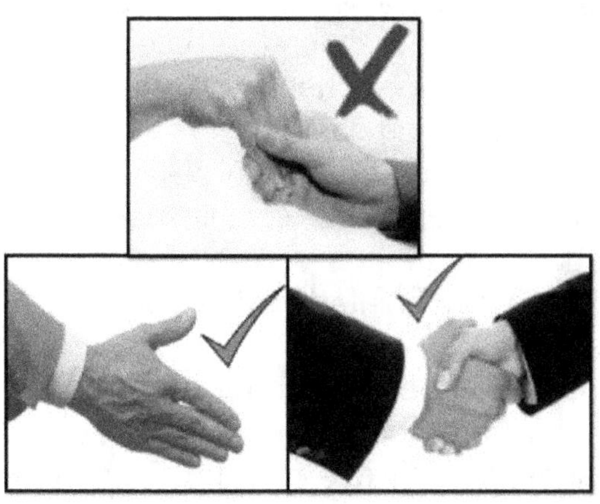

While it is good to give the other person a firm handshake, it is also important to note that 'firm' should not mean 'bone-crushing' but just comfortable enough for the other person. In other words your handshake should convey 'CARE'!

(Think of: **CAIR**- **C**onfidence, **A**ssurance, **I**nterest, **R**espect)

That is why we recommend that you practice the exact firmness of your handshake first with your own hand. This could be done by taking your left hand out: 4 fingers together and thumb up with the hand facing inwards towards you, as if it is a customers' hand. Now take your right hand the usual way you would use to shake someone's hand and assuming that your left hand is your customers' hand, shake as follows: Web into web first followed by the 4 fingers of your right hand around your left hand, with the thumb finally locking. Basically 3 locks...web into web, 4 fingers around and thumbs interlocked. Since it is your own hand, you will know what amount of firmness to use.

Keep practicing till you are comfortable with the right amount of firmness to clasp the other person's hand without it being 'bone-crushing' or the opposite- too limp (a dead fish hand shake!)

You can do this exercise whenever you are free, till you get accustomed to the exact amount of pressure to be used.

Now for some key points to remember while shaking hands:

A handshake can be initiated by either person and is appropriate when meeting a business associate in a social setting. Always stand when shaking someone's hand, and step out from behind a desk or table, while maintaining good eye contact and posture. A handshake should end by the time you have finished greeting the person. When meeting an elderly or disabled person, allow them to initiate the handshake.

Business Card Etiquette

When presenting business cards, they must always be presented face up with the front portion of the card facing towards the customer/guest, and if presenting with one hand as in most western countries then it must be held by the tip not covering any part of the text on the card.

Most Asian countries present cards with both hands. Whatever be the culture, please ensure the cards are never kept in a wallet as they would tend to get folded or bent at the edges or corner. All cards must be in pristine condition, crisp with no folds, wrinkles or soggy edges. Whenever presenting the card, make eye contact, with a pleasant smile.

Remembering Names

One of the most embarrassing moments when introducing people, would be when you mess up on their names. Remembering names may be difficult for some people, but it's not impossible. It's a skill: something that you can improve with constant practice and application.

Here are some ways to remember names:

- ✓ Repeat: When someone is introduced to you, repeat their name. "It's a pleasure to meet you, John." This can help reinforce your memory of the name. You may also introduce them to someone else so that you can create an opportunity to use their name.
- ✓ Use mental imagery: We think in pictures, therefore associating an image with a name can help in assisting recall. Imagine a

person's name written on their forehead. Pick an imagery that works for you. The more striking or exaggerated your mental picture, the bigger are the chances of recall.

✓ Put it on paper: Write the name down as soon as you can. Write their details on the business card they give you so that you would remember them the next time you see them around. (But make sure you don't let the person see you writing on their business card.)

✓ Be genuinely interested: Remembering names begin with attitude. If you are sincerely interested in a person, then they would make an impact on you. If you adapt the attitude that everyone is interesting, and are a potential ally in business, then remembering names would come as second nature.

Positive Introductions: Protocol, Rank, Status, Titles and Forms of Address

The first rule for introductions is that they be made. Don't get too worried about making a mistake during the introduction. Forgoing an introduction altogether, however, is a mistake that may leave a negative impression. Remember, as seen earlier, First Impressions create lasting Impressions. With that said, we must realize that the goal for making introductions is to provide information about each other so that there is a common ground to carry on a conversation. Introducing people is one of the most important acts we experience doing in our daily lives, yet very few people know how to do it correctly. Knowing how to make a graceful introduction will not only allow you to make a good impression but it will also give you the confidence and power to nurture these relationships from the get-go.

Studies have found that most people would rather have you ask for their names than to stand in a group and not be introduced. Another equally embarrassing scenario that often takes place is when it's 'assumed' two persons know one another and the introduction may go something like, "You two know one another." It is for this reason, at many business and/or social functions name badges are provided. They are given for the simple reason to help your memory.

To start, here are some important business introduction etiquette rules to remember:

There are five "S"s to a great introduction:

1. Smile.
2. Stand up straight.
3. See: make eye contact
4. Shake hands.
5. Say: "Hi! My name is ...and I don't think we've met…

Arrival and Greetings when meeting someone
- ✓ As mentioned above, keep the 5S's in mind
- ✓ Repeat the other person's name in your greeting. Then say the name several times during the conversation
- ✓ Both men and women should be ready to initiate the handshake.
- ✓ Do not remove your jacket unless the host does. If you are uncomfortable, you may ask the host(s) permission to remove your jacket.
- ✓ It is considered acceptable for men to assist women with their chair but it does not always

happen; in upscale restaurants, wait staff may assist.
- ✓ Another rule of thumb is that you're not expected when leaving an event to tour the entire room like a politician. It's always proper to say goodbye to those nearest to you and always seek out the host of the evening

When being Introduced
- ✓ When introducing yourself or when being introduced always stand and extend your right hand.
- ✓ If the person you're meeting is much older or a higher- level executive, say, *"I'm happy to meet you, Mr./ Ms. Name,'* or *"How do you do, Mr./ Mrs. Name,"*
- ✓ You may usually call younger people by their first names.
- ✓ If someone says, "How do you do," in response to an introduction, the proper response is, "How do you do" or "Pleased to meet you" and not 'fine thank you' as " How do you do" is a greeting, <u>not</u> a question.
- ✓ Say "I'm pleased to meet you" in response to an introduction. If you are being introduced, stand unless you are physically unable to.
- ✓ "Hello Mr./ Ms. Jackson. It's so very nice to meet you". Continue to use proper names when addressing your host until they give you permission to call them by their first name.
- ✓ If, however, you were introduced earlier in the evening and had some conversation, upon departure it is OK to say, "I'm glad to have met you Tom" Or, If you're on the receiving end of

the farewell, reply "Thank you, Tom" or "I also enjoyed talking with you."
- ✓ If you are introducing more than one person, add a small amount of information about each person (any mutual interests you are aware of, how you know them, or their occupation). This gives them a starting point for a conversation.
- ✓ Always have business cards on hand.

What do you say when you meet someone? Introducing Yourself

If you introduce yourself to another person, provide them with both your last and first names. The other person may have an easier time remembering your name if you give them a small piece of information about yourself on what you do etc.

Always have your Elevator Speech ready! Here are some examples:

Good Afternoon, I am Gerard Assey and the Founder CEO of a Group: 'Citius, Altius, Fortius Unlimited, specialising in Corporate Training, one of the divisions being the only one in this part of the World to be listed under the 'Who's Who of Training' and ranked as No.1 on all search engines!

Good morning, my name is Philip Johnson. My company, PJ Display Products, offers convenient, lightweight trade show displays to make your booth setup easier"

Now take a few minutes and work on preparing your own unique introduction!

When Introducing Others

- ✓ When you introduce someone, start with *"Mr. A, I'd like you to please meet Mr. B from Company / Dept / Location,"* or *Mrs. B, I'd like*

*to introduce my sister, and C. C, this is Mrs.
B."*

- ✓ Never phrase an introduction as a command: *"Mr. A, shake hands with / meet Ms. B."*
- ✓ Next, say something about the person being introduced: *"Ms. B works in our Marketing Division; or "John is a former neighbor of ours at (Location)."*
- ✓ This little bit of information to the group about the newcomer provides a topic of discussion so that the conversation can flow smoothly.
- ✓ Refrain however, from long stories about how you met, or about the person's life or background.
- ✓ Avoid phrases of superiority like *"John works for me"*

Protocol in Business Etiquette

- ✓ Generally, a lower ranked person in business is introduced to the higher ranked person - not vice versa. (Executives, clients, important guests would fall into the "higher ranked person" category.)
- ✓ When introducing a younger person to an older person (Use younger person's first name, elder's Last - about 15 years is the deciding point.) The name to say first is the Older person's ("Ms. D, this is Jonny Alexander.") Typically, someone younger is introduced to someone older.
- ✓ When a client is visiting, everyone in the office is introduced to the client first.
- ✓ When introducing a Peer in your firm to an outsider, the name to say first is the outsider's. When a peer from another company is

introduced to a peer from your company, the person from your company is introduced to the person from the other company first.

- ✓ When introducing a non official to an official, always say the Officials name first
- ✓ When introducing a junior executive to a senior executive, always say the Senior Executive's name first.
- ✓ When introducing a company executive to a customer or a client, always say the clients name first
- ✓ A family member is introduced first to your boss.
- ✓ At an event with a guest of honor, all other guests are introduced first to the guest of honor.
- ✓ Always present the senior citizen, guest of honor, or dignitary first. Be sure to use titles, not first names, when introducing a much older person, a doctor (physician, psychologist, veterinarian, Ph.D.), a member of the clergy, or someone of official rank.
- ✓ Use a dignitary's title even if that person is retired and no longer holds that position: "Governor Singh," "Mayor Abraham," "Colonel Johnson," "Ambassador Kapoor."
- ✓ An obvious breach of etiquette is calling someone by a name you prefer, not the name they prefer. An unflattering nickname has no place in business .If Charles prefers to be called "Charles," that's what you should call him and how you should introduce him - not as "Charlie" or "Chuck." If you don't call him by the right name, or if you mispronounce his

name, it's acceptable for Charles to correct you.
- ✓ If Charles prefers to be called "Chuckie boy," that's his business. Don't assume, however, that you know what people prefer.
- ✓ People are very sensitive about their names. Using incorrect names hurts your credibility and your chance of doing business with those you've misnamed.

Here are some examples that you can use to practice:

Situation 1 - Boss to Client
1. Introducer
2. Client: Mr. Samson
3. Your boss: Ms. Jackson

The introducer would say to the client, Mr. Samson, I'd like to introduce to you Ms. Jackson. Ms. Jackson is our Country Head. Mr. Samson is our client from Mauritius.

Situation 2 - Executive to a Client
1. Introducer
2. Office Manager: Susie Thomas
3. Client: Sanjay Kumar

The introducer would say to the client, Mr. Kumar, I'd like to introduce to you Susie Thomas. Ms. Thomas is our Sales Manager. Mr. Kumar is our client from Singapore

Situation 3- Junior Executive to Senior Executive
1. Introducer
2. Sr. Executive
3. Jr. Executive

The introducer would say to the Sr. Executive, Mr. Xxxx (Sr. Executive's name), I'd like to introduce to you Mr. Yyyy (Jr. Executive's name)

Overcoming Introduction Slip-ups
- ✓ Forgetting Names: Forgetting a person's name whom you have met before can happen to all of us and the worst thing you can do is to ignore them and not introduce them to your friends. The best thing to do is to apologize and say, "I am sorry, I know we have met but I can't remember your name." or say "I'm having a difficult time remembering your name." They should say their name and then you introduce everyone.
- ✓ Far ruder than forgetting a name, is not introducing people at all. People are usually very uncomfortable when they're not introduced as part of the group.
- ✓ When you're expecting several people and they are arriving separately, introduce each person as he or she arrives. Just politely interrupt the group's conversation and introduce the newcomer: "I'd like you all to meet Amanda Peters, the Communication Expert. Amanda, these are our associates from the southeastern office: Raj Sharma, Susan Abraham, and Mathew Thomas."
- ✓ If you're the one who's not introduced, take the initiative. Don't call attention and don't ask for an introduction. Just stand, extend your hand, smile and say, "Good Afternoon. I'm John Mathew, Mr. Fernando's Secretary and PA."

- ✓ If you are introduced but others are not, you may certainly take the initiative now, it's perfectly acceptable to start the conversation by introducing.
- ✓ There will be times when you do not remember everyone's name in the group- the best option in this case is to suggest that the people introduce themselves.
- ✓ If you are in a group and someone new walks up and no one introduces them, the polite thing to do is to stick out your hand and begin by saying your name. When this happens, it is a clue that the person you are with has forgotten the new person's name and can't introduce you.
- ✓ Not knowing one another: When you do not know if the people know one another, ask- "Have you met before?" If you are being introduced and the person doing the introductions hesitates, fill in the introduction details.

Saying Good bye

- ✓ When escorting your guests back to the main exit, thank them for coming, shake each person's hand firmly, and make good eye contact.
- ✓ Just remember that the main rule of good manners in greeting people and making introductions is consideration for everyone.
- ✓ Even if you don't know the precise etiquettes, if you put people at ease and show proper respect, your actions will be acceptable.

Manners and Etiquette at the Workplace

"Manners are the happy way of doing things; each one a stroke of genius, or of love, now repeated and hardened into usage." Ralph Waldo Emerson

When it comes to working in an office or other professional setting, etiquette and your manners matter a lot. How you present yourself and interact with others around you- your coworkers, bosses, or the ones that report to you- speaks of who you are as a person and can directly influence the trajectory of your career and credibility.

More so these days, is etiquette so important to professional success, as it can establish respect amongst colleagues, seniors and your subordinates. When you utilize proper manners, you nurture a collaborative environment. As a result, each team member can feel heard, understood, and integral to fulfilling the company's goals. The goal of business etiquette is to present a united company image, foster mutual respect for team members, and improve communication in the workplace, which in turn will enhance the image and credibility of the organization. And when all this happens, they do better work.

So here are some quick Do's and Don'ts for the Workplace:

- ✓ Do arrive early. Try to never be late: Being on time and punctual in a work environment shows that you respect everyone's schedule.
- ✓ Greet others irrespective of position or title: When you present a friendly demeanor in your

workplace, it can help others feel more comfortable, which may encourage them to ask you for assistance or advice.

✓ Be respectful to your coworkers: All your colleagues deserve respect, even if they are not respectful towards you. A respectful attitude is a must in workplace etiquette because it increases your productivity and collaboration and also gives you a different level of satisfaction.

✓ Dress appropriately for the office: This will depend on the particular culture of your workplace. But it's always a good idea to dress to impress, especially when you're first starting a new role at a company, otherwise no one will take you seriously if you don't.

✓ Show up to work clean and well-groomed: Prioritize proper hygiene by maintaining a clean and neat appearance.

✓ Stay home when you're sick: To keep your workplace healthy and avoid spreading germs, stay at home if you don't feel well.

✓ Try to always have a smile: Having a positive attitude about being at work will affect your job performance significantly. Appearing happy, friendly, and approachable at work can do wonders for your career. Never underestimate the power of a smile!

✓ Have a "can-do" attitude. Work ethic, the willingness to take on challenges, and displayed creativeness will improve your reputation in the office.

✓ Remember names: Greeting people correctly, using their right names is yet, another important office etiquette, and for that, you need to remember people's names. You can create a mental picture that can help you recall their name, and repeating the person's name several times can also be beneficial in remembering names.

- ✓ Knock First: Take the time to knock first before barging in directly, demonstrates respect for the person on the other side of the door.
- ✓ Never interrupt others or meetings: When people are focused on discussing a topic it is only polite to wait until they are finished- wait until the meeting is finished to interrupt.
- ✓ Honor your commitments/Keep you Word: If you are continually accountable for your assignments and other commitments, it will show that you are a responsible person. So work on meeting deadlines, as this sends an unspoken message of respect for your responsibilities, as well as the value you place on the time and commitments
- ✓ Avoid speaking loudly: Speak quietly. Be aware of your surroundings. When you're on the phone, conversing in the hallway, or visiting a coworker at their cubicle, be sensitive to others working and speak quietly.
- ✓ Silence your notifications: When you work in a shared space, turn off notifications on your phone, email and messaging services to minimize noise.
- ✓ Don't bring your emotions into the office: It's best to leave your personal emotions at the door when you get to work. If you truly can't focus on your work because something has happened, it's probably a better idea to take some personal time to process your emotions.

Or, if something in the workplace is bothering you, reach out to your supervisor to resolve the issue so it doesn't interfere with your work

✓ Do be willing to help out a coworker: This is an opportunity to stand out and demonstrate your own knowledge and skills. It's also an opportunity to make a friend and bring someone into your corner for the future; you never know when that might come in handy.

✓ Stay flexible: Adjusting well to change shows that you are a team player and are willing to do what's best for the company.

✓ Respect shared spaces: The way you treat shared spaces will reflect on you as a professional, so it's important that you label things correctly, stay organized, and respect others who also use these spaces. Business etiquette applies to shared spaces whether you're cleaning up after yourself physically or following company processes online.

✓ Keep the workplace clean

✓ Share credit when appropriate: If you're part of a group project, make sure all team members receive recognition for their work. This shows teamwork and honesty.

✓ Respond to phone calls, messages, voice mails promptly.

✓ Follow the etiquette for your Phone (including your mobile phone), Email or Video calling (More on each of these under a separate chapter)

✓ Avoid Gossip: How you treat people speaks a lot about you, so don't indulge in rumors about other staff in the office. Engaging in office gossip can come and haunt you back someday. So remember that every word you speak reflects your personality, both personally and professionally.

✓ Try to do more of listening than talking: It shows you care and can help you gain a lot.

✓ Think before you speak: The workplace can sometimes be a stressful and challenging environment, with each person having a different personality and perspective towards their work and thus clashes can happen at the workplace. The easiest thing you can do to maintain a healthy and productive workplace is to think before you speak. Once a harsh word gets out, you can never withdraw it. So be cautious and think before you speak.

✓ In a business setting, women and men are colleagues. Men should avoid following traditional etiquette customs-such as pulling out chairs, opening doors, helping with coats, or carrying packages. However, proper etiquette still requires that a person (regardless of gender) arriving at a door first should open it. If you notice someone (regardless of gender) carrying something heavy or cumbersome as they approach a door, offer aid.

✓ Keep personal matters totally off or to a minimum: Because the overall goal of workplace etiquette is to be respectful of your organization and your coworkers, you'll want to avoid things that might interfere with anyone's productivity. Also, remember that personal business doesn't just include phone calls or conversations about your life outside of work. These days, it's easier than ever to take a quick break by whipping out your phone to peruse social media. But what you intended to be a five-minute distraction can quickly turn into 20 minutes of wasted time.

Handling the Boss

- ✓ Remember that your boss always gets the last word-wrong or right.
- ✓ Do your best to inform your boss. You don't want to put your boss surprised with good or bad information from an unwanted source.
- ✓ Do not go over your boss' head. Undermining your boss without letting her or him know what you are doing is a good way to sabotage your own career.
- ✓ Use your best effort to make your boss look good. Making your boss look good will be appreciated and lead to your future success.

Departmental Meetings

- ✓ Always arrive on time.
- ✓ Read the agenda ahead of time and come prepared. Where or what areas can you contribute into the meeting.
- ✓ Come well dressed- in proper business attire
- ✓ Maintain eye contact with the speaker.
- ✓ Sit up straight.
- ✓ Treat everyone equally; don't treat the top management special while ignoring others.
- ✓ Plan to say at least one thing, or ask one question.
- ✓ If you're leading the meeting, circulate an agenda well in advance, so others can be prepared.

- ✓ Put all the action items first. Then, discussion other points if time permits.
- ✓ Stick to the schedule.
- ✓ Give everyone a chance to speak. Do not allow domination of a few.
- ✓ At all times maintain courtesy
- ✓ Have minutes of meeting recorded and follow for action

Eating at the Office

These days, eating at one's desk is becoming an increasingly part of the office environment. If you do eat at your workspace, here are some business dining etiquette tips to keep in mind to avoid offending your coworkers.

- ✓ Don't Mess/Clutter. Keep it clean. If you eat at your desk, keep some wipes nearby and wipe it down afterwards.
- ✓ Smell. Avoid eating pungent foods at work.
- ✓ Location. Eat in the break room, cafeteria or an outdoor space if available (avoid eating at your desk if possible).
- ✓ And if you have an office, keep the door closed.
    - Don't eat in front of customers.
    - Don't eat while walking in the halls or corridors.
- ✓ Eat before the start time of your work. Many people are under the impression that the first few minutes of the day is meant for them to have a cup of coffee and snack to eat at their desk. This can eat into your work time. So always eat before settling in for the day.
- ✓ Noise. Don't chew by making a loud noise or smack your lips or burping.

- ✓ Socialize. Take advantage of the occasional lunchtime with coworkers to socialize.
- ✓ Gargle your Mouth/ Freshen up. Brush your teeth after eating and make sure you look fresh.

Office Furniture and Desk Privacy

- ✓ Treat the furniture well: Do not put your feet on the furniture.
- ✓ Avoid scribbling on desks, walls or other office property
- ✓ Do not sit at another's desk or use their computer without permission.
- ✓ If a piece of furniture is moved to another place for a few minutes (with permission off course), ensure the same is placed back after use
- ✓ Don't eat or drink if what is in the office refrigerator isn't yours!
- ✓ Never use someone else's cell phone without permission.
- ✓ Never ever pry into some else's cell phone- messages, photos etc
- ✓ When dealing with your visitors, is it appropriate for you to meet with the person in this venue? Think!

Office Parties

- ✓ Office parties are good opportunities to improve morale and build good will. Do not decline the invitation to attend an office party; not attending could hurt your reputation.
- ✓ Don't pull the nightclub attire from your closet for the event- ask whether the attire for the party is formal or casual.

- ✓ Keep in mind these are people who see you every day and they will remember a lapse in behavior. Act as though your behavior is being observed every minute (because it probably is).
- ✓ Be aware of your alcoholic consumption. After what goes in you may not have control of what you say. So do not embarrass yourself.
- ✓ Do not discuss business - this is a social occasion and an opportunity to learn more about your co-workers.
- ✓ Don't use the office party as an excuse to blow off steam.
- ✓ Keep your hands to yourself. Don't flirt, and avoid any other inappropriate behavior.
- ✓ Keep one hand free during the night so you can offer handshakes to people as they come by.
- ✓ Don't forget to thank the person responsible for the planning and coordinating of the party. Consider sending a thank-you note to top management for hosting the party.

Car and Taxi Business Travel Etiquette

- ✓ Company Car: Keep your car clean; it represents you and the company.
- ✓ Never drink and drive. Drive responsibly and courteously. At many companies, speeding tickets can result in a bad image and ban from driving the company car.
- ✓ Even if there is one passenger as a non-smoker, there should be no smoking in the vehicle. If traveling with a smoker, the driver should offer to periodically stop for smoke breaks.

✓ If your company requires, keep legible, accurate and organized records of mileage and destinations. Unless specified or permitted do not use your company car for personal use
✓ If it is a chauffeur driven vehicle, greet the driver as you enter the car. If you are traveling by taxi with a group of business colleagues, proper etiquette dictates that senior colleagues be offered a seat in the back (unless they prefer to ride in front).
✓ Tip generously and request a receipt for your records.

Air Travel Business Etiquette

✓ For travel during working hours, dress in business attire. If traveling outside of business hours, business casual is appropriate.
✓ Treat flight attendants with respect. Avoid using the call bell if possible. Make requests as the attendants are passing by instead. Ask politely, and say thank-you. Greet them as you enter and offer a good-bye as you exit the plane.
✓ Once seated and buckled in, avoid unnecessary trips out of your seat. If you anticipate having to frequently leave your seat during a flight, make sure to book an aisle seat.
✓ Keep in mind that some other travelers may enjoy a good conversation during the flight but others may not. So before striking up a conversation, evaluate your travel companion's body language. If you begin a conversation and their responses are short

and they ask no questions or thoughts, end the discussion.

✓ Remember to keep detailed expense records during your business trip. Request receipts for each service you receive. Using one credit card makes tracking expenses easier. Apps that help track expenses can also be helpful.

✓ Never puff up a bill by adding extra amounts for a meal or additional mileage to get more. That is unethical and can affect your credibility and can even cause you to lose your job

Managing Relationships: The Right Questions and Listening are KEYS!

Learning to ask better questions in our everyday conversations has enormous benefits on relationships. Firstly, asking appreciative questions improves one's emotional intelligence and demonstrates empathy to the receiver of your question. Also, asking well-considered questions expands the possibilities in the answer and has the potential to deepen a relationship.
However, sadly, we are biased towards telling instead of asking, because we live in a pragmatic, problem-solving culture in which knowing things and telling others what we know is valued. In order to build relationships based on dialogue and mutual respect, it is essential to learn to ask more questions. This shows care and concern.

Questions are a powerful tool to nurture relationships and make them effective and satisfactory for both sides.

If we start asking more questions we will immediately notice the benefits in our relationships with others:
- ✓ We'll understand the people we are relating to
- ✓ We'll focus on them and encourage empathy
- ✓ We'll allow them to express themselves and give us the information we want
- ✓ We'll stimulate their attention and their involvement
- ✓ It would indicate that we care and are genuinely concerned.

In order that the communicative exchange is effective and that the dialogue is fluid, it is important to ask the right question, and in order to ask our questions in an effective way, we should ask ourselves *"What do I want to obtain? What do I really need to know?"* This way the exchange of information can go straight to the point

So the art of asking the right questions requires the use of different types of questions. First let us have an understanding of the different types of questions that we could ask someone. Though there are several types of questions, for the purpose of this exercise let us look at just the 3 most important ones ie;

OPEN Questions

CLOSED Questions

FOLLOW-UP Questions

Depending on what type of answer you want from the other person, either of these questions are used.

Eg; If I asked you: *'Did you have your dinner'?*

Or *'Do you like this training session?'* or *'Are you going home this evening'?*

The only possible answer that you could give me would either be a *'yes'* or a *'no'*

That is why this type of question is called a 'closed question', because the only possible answer would be a one word- with either a *'yes'* or *'no'*

Closed questions usually begin with:

'Are you…'

'Will you…'

'Do you…'

'Would you…'

They are usually not very helpful in starting a conversation and extracting information. However, most people are more comfortable asking such questions.

The opposite of 'closed' is the obvious: 'open'. Open questions allow the other person to open up or do the talking and are used to encourage the other side to speak freely about a concern or expand on something already raised during the conversation.

Always remember this: Open questions generally begin with 5W's and 1 H ie;

Who?

What?

When?

Where?

Why?

How?

And they encourage the other person to open up and speak.

If we were to redo that example again using open questions, they would go something like this: *'What did you have for dinner?' 'How do you feel about this training?' 'What plans do you have for this evening'?*

These questions will certainly not fetch you a *'yes'* or *'no'* like how closed questions do. But they would allow the other person to open up with information which is what we could be looking forward to, by asking such questions.

Shooting out these questions without any logical order would also be inappropriate, as it could be unprofessional, could be irritating at times and most of all cause confusion in the mind of the other person. But if the other person was taken through a logical pattern, it could help lead him or open up to making the conversation two-way and interesting for both parties

Effective listening involves the use of follow-up questions and they are useful in several ways:

- ✓ They show we are interested and encourage the other person to keep talking.
- ✓ They increase the quality of the information gained.
- ✓ They help us to confirm our understanding of what has been said.

Before we can ask a follow-up question we need to listen to what the other side has said and wait for an appropriate pause in the conversation to ask the question.

Follow-up questions can also take the form of a question asked in response to a statement by the other side. They can reflect the information in the original question by beginning with phrases like:

So you are saying that...?

Does that mean...?

If I understand correctly are you saying that...?

Followed by a summary of what was said by the other person.

Let us see some examples now!

Examples of Open questions:

What exactly do you see the issue as Tim?

How can I help you solve this problem?

These Questions can help to dig into or search for details and are also called Probing Questions:

"Exactly how did this happen?"

"What steps did you take?"

Examples of Closed questions:

Did you receive the letter we sent you on Friday?

Are you happy with the service you have received?

Examples of Follow up questions:
What were you told when you rang us?
How quickly were you promised a reply?
In these examples the follow-up questions have been asked in response to the customer saying that he
1) Rang us previously,
2) Was told he would be given a reply

Listening Skills
Now while the other person talks, you would need to listen attentively.
'People were designed with two ears and one mouth, and that is the ratio in which to use them'!
How to be a good listener?
One of the greatest skills that one can develop is the skill of listening. The best professionals are the ones that do less talking and more of listening and that is why I believe God gave us two ears and one mouth- so we would do more listening than talking!

Listen Actively
- ✓ Focus on the speaker
- ✓ Keep an open mind
- ✓ Tolerate silence
- ✓ Ask open-ended questions
- ✓ Repeat the speaker's thoughts
- ✓ Listen for facts and key words

To be an "active" listener:
- ✓ Suspend judgment, initially
- ✓ Avoid distractions; when on the telephone don't carry on side conversations; when face-to-face make eye contact
- ✓ Assess what you heard
- ✓ Clarify and confirm

✓ Take notes of key points
✓ Never use your phone in the other's premises, particularly a customer! It's a big disturbance and bad manners!

Before you respond, assess the information you heard by asking yourself four questions:
✓ What has he/she told me?
✓ What can I do with this information?
✓ What else do I need to know?
✓ What questions do I still need to ask?

To show you're listening actively:
✓ Use terms like, 'Go on', Uh huh' and 'mmm'
✓ Stay tuned in/Watch for non-verbal cues

To show that you have, understood:
✓ Use, phrases like "I see," "I understand"
✓ Paraphrase, "So you want me to …"

Clarifying what they said:
In order to more fully understand what is being said we can make it clearer by asking for more detail:
✓ *You said that you were not satisfied with our service...Can you tell me why?*
✓ *You mentioned how helpful we had been. Can you elaborate specifically in what way?*
✓ *You said there had been problems in the past. What were they like?*

Clarifying and Reconfirming with Closed Questions

This is the time when closed questions are very useful. To clarify and reconfirm, restate in your own words what the other person has said and ask him/her to verify your understanding. An example would be: *'Mr Customer, Let me just take a minute to summarize, just to ensure that I've got the right information…You were mentioning that you were having a problem with….Am I right Mr. So & So?"*

After the other person has confirmed your understanding, you have earned the right to proceed with additional questions to gain more information about the situation.

Why summarize regularly?

- *It keeps complexities under control*
- *It tests progress*
- *It lets you restate what the other party has said*
- *It can help gain the initiative*
- *It can keep the discussion on track*
- *It can prevent misinterpretation, misunderstanding and subsequent bitterness*
- *In other words, summarizing helps you stay on top (but you take the point).*

By summarizing, you are making sure you have the right information and that you haven't left out anything.

Telephone Skills and Manners

The telephone is such a powerful tool today, but the problem with telephones is that people can't be impressed by the size of your office, the smile on your face, or the clothes you're wearing. They have only two things to go by- your **Attitude** and your **Voice**. People who call your office only once will base 90 percent of what they think of your company on that one call.

Providing Exceptional Service on the Telephone
- ✓ The phone's every ring means business in one way or another, so make sure you are treating it like the sales-boosting tool it can be!
- ✓ Treat EVERY call importantly
- ✓ Every time you make or receive a telephone call at work, you're **representing** your company. The impression you create can be a lasting one so make sure your voice and manner always show you in the best and most professional light.
- ✓ When someone feels you're giving him/her personal consideration, they'll have more confidence in you and your company.

Here are some ways that can help you be more professional on the phone:
- ✓ Smile! It will show out in your voice
- ✓ Picking a ringing phone! 1st, 2nd or 3rd ring?
- ✓ Answering your phone: What to say? Greet/ Salutation, your name, department, company name
- ✓ Always begin a call by introducing yourself and identifying your company.

- ✓ Right tone: Project confidence- Make sure your voice exudes strength and power
- ✓ React/ Respond to the other person's conversation: *"Yes, I see, I agree…"*
- ✓ End on a positive note: *(I enjoyed speaking with you Ms. …" or "Thanks so much for your time, Mr… I look forward to meeting you soon.")*
- ✓ Hang up after the caller, leaving the receiver quietly down.
- ✓ Taking messages: Accuracy/ Spell/ Repeat
- ✓ Call back as promised or have someone do so!
- ✓ Always ask the caller if he/she would like to hold. Avoid the abrupt phrase *"hold please."*
- ✓ Let the caller know how long it will take and ask whether he/she prefers to hold or be called back.
- ✓ Update the caller periodically (possibly every 2 minutes). Be as specific as you can be.
- ✓ If you are so busy that the call cannot be handled in an efficient manner, give the caller an option of being called back
- ✓ If someone calls you while you are on another call, tell your caller you will call him back. *"Good Morning Mr. Jackson, I'm on the other line. May I get back to you in just a few minutes?"* This way, poor Mr. Harry isn't left listening to a dead receiver on the other line. Because Mr. Harry might hang up on you or be unresponsive the next time you call.
- ✓ The person you called always has priority.

If you are handling or receiving a call for someone else, then:
- ✓ Never demand *"Who is calling?"* Better: *"May I tell him who is calling?"*
- ✓ Never tell a caller *"He has left for the day…or at the canteen"*. Always: *"He is unavailable at this moment, can I take a message"* or *"May I tell him what you're calling about…maybe I might be able to help!"* (Always show concern!)

  "Ms. XYZ is out at the moment, but she should be back soon. Would you like to hold or may I ask her to return your call"?

  OR

  "Ms. ABC is on another line; would you like to hold?"
- ✓ If the caller agrees to hold, remember to return to the line and ask him/her if he/she would like to continue to hold.

When you call others
- ✓ Do have a written outline or plan of the topics you want to discuss
- ✓ Do leave a brief message if the person does not answer (State your name, reason for the call and the message, telephone number to call back, best time for the return call)
- ✓ Do ask if the person has time to talk. If he or she is busy, set up a time to call back
- ✓ Do call the person back if you get disconnected.
- ✓ Do not eat while on the phone
- ✓ Do not talk to others while they are on the phone
- ✓ Do not be the first to hang up, and do hang up gently

When others call you:
- ✓ Do try to answer the phone within three rings
- ✓ Do not say 'Hello'. Use a salutation followed by your name, department, and organization
- ✓ If people are calling you at a bad time, do explain and offer to call back
- ✓ Do not take multiple calls at one time, keeping people on hold. Do let the voice mail take a message and call back
- ✓ Do keep paper and pencil ready

5 Phases of a Call

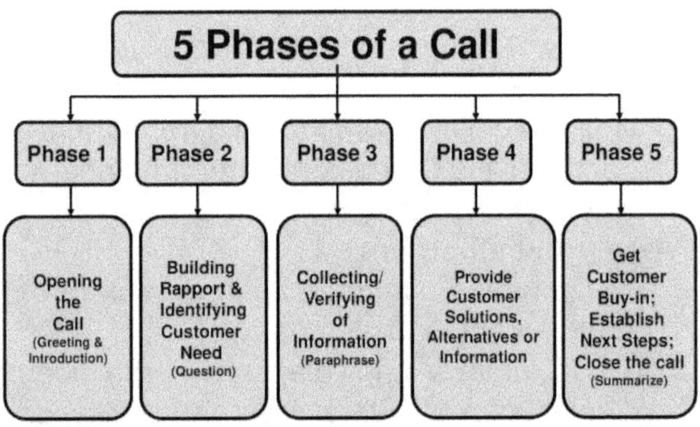

Incoming Calls- Call Structure

The general structure for incoming calls should be:
- ✓ Open and introduction
- ✓ Ask questions / Listen/ Notes/ Clarify
- ✓ Identify the problem
- ✓ Recommend a solution
- ✓ Commitment to further action
- ✓ Close the call

Outgoing Calls-Call Structure
The structure should be:
- ✓ Plan and prepare-Keep outline ready
- ✓ Open and introduction
- ✓ Ask questions/ Listen/ Notes/ Clarify
- ✓ Confirm your understanding of the problem
- ✓ Recommend a solution
- ✓ Commitment to further action
- ✓ Close the call

Speakerphone Etiquette
Always let the people whom you are talking to know that they are on a speakerphone. If it's possible, ask them if they mind being placed on speaker before switching to speakerphone. Keep outside noises to a minimum. It is not appropriate to place on speakerphone without the permission of the other side

Voicemail Etiquette
Return messages as promptly as possible, wait no longer than one business day at the longest.
If you know you will be unable to return an outgoing message within one business day, record a message letting callers know what dates you will or provide an alternate number if you can. But make sure your outgoing message is brief and professional.
If leaving a message, provide:
- ✓ Your name;
- ✓ Your number;
- ✓ The date of your call;
- ✓ Whether you anticipate calling back; and
- ✓ A brief reason for the call

Taking a Message-Establishing the details:
Find out:
- The name of the caller
- Their organization
- Their contact details
- A time when they can be contacted
- The message
- Specific action required
- Repeat this information back to the caller
- Double-check spellings and contact details

Remember that customers form a mental '**PICTURE**' of you from the following:
P-Pitch
I-Inflection
C-Courtesy
T-Tone
U-Understanding
R-Rate
E-Enunciation

Cell Phone Etiquette

Remember that during business hours, business comes first. Your number one priority should be to give the people around you courtesy and respect.
Here are some Do's and Don'ts:
- ✓ In the office, make sure your phone is on silent or vibration mode. Turn your phone to vibrate in public places such as movie theaters, religious services, restaurants, etc. And do it before your phone rings
- ✓ Talk as quietly as possible. Cell phones today have very sensitive microphones and speakers- you don't have to yell to be heard.

- ✓ Try not to use an inappropriate song ring tone and opt for a conservative ringer
- ✓ Do not share your "business" with everyone around you. They do not want to hear about your latest argument with your boss, friend, wife, husband, your mom or others. Keep private conversations private! You never know who is within hearing distance.
- ✓ If you are expecting an important call that you have to take (like from your customer!) let your host/ boss/friends know ahead of time. Excuse yourself when the call comes in; respect the people you are with-they should be more important than the calls you want to make or receive.
- ✓ Never yell or show anger when speaking on a cell phone
- ✓ Don't bring your cell phone into the restroom... Ever!
- ✓ Don't bring your cell phone to meetings as it may tempt you to text or peep into messages during the less interesting moments.
- ✓ When walking and talking on your cell phone, be aware of your surroundings and remember to respect the rights of others

The Internet-One Last Caution! The Internet is the world's largest brain, that is always active and it never forgets anything ever. Once something gets onto it and released into the wild, it's potentially there in some form forever. So think before you put up anything…Never put anything up online that you wouldn't let your family read

E-Mail Etiquette

There is little doubt that online technologies have transformed the way business operates in recent years. And in this age of such advanced technology, email is still the most preferred and often most efficient form of communication, but yet regrettably many organizations treat this very important form of business communication casually and lightly.

With the average professional sending an average of 40 emails per day and receiving 121, there is definitely a chance to move fast in email communication, thus overlooking fundamental email etiquette rules. This means that you have 40 opportunities to market yourself and your business in those individual emails you send, every single day.

A recent study found that the average adult spends approximately 5 hours a day checking email: 3 hours checking work email and 2 hours checking personal email. This time is spent reading and composing hundreds of messages at a very fast pace- obviously leaving a lot of room for error. These errors can lead to missed opportunities or appearing totally unprofessional.

You would have experienced many replying to emails late or not at all or even sending replies that do not actually answer the questions being asked. This can cause a potentially damaging effect on the image of the organization, resulting finally in a loss of business.

As we've seen earlier, there are basically 3 key entrances to any business:

1. The front door (face- to-face-walk-in-customers or customers solicited by your sales personnel)

2. The telephone and

3. The net. And the chances are that, if either of these are NOT handled properly, you have lost your customer forever!

Think of this for a moment: If most of the business coming in is through the net, and if your organization is able to deal professionally with email, then this will most certainly result in your organization having that all important competitive edge. On the other hand, if not handled the right way, then in the very first instance, chances are that you have lost a customer- and it could even be forever. And remember word of mouth travels fast today- thanks to the social media platforms.

Therefore, when it comes to any material or correspondence being sent out from your organization, it is of vital importance to convey the right message in the right way- to ensure that this creates the right impression that you are a credible, professional enterprise and one that will be easy and a pleasure to do business with. And remember you only have that one chance to make that first impression which will be invaluable to building trust and confidence.

So here are some quick Do's and Don'ts that you might like to keep in mind:

Do's

1. **Do use only a business email address**: If you work for an organization, then you've probably been assigned a business email address with your company's domain. If that's the case, you should use it for all of your business correspondence, even if you prefer your personal email address or mail client. Using your business email doesn't just look

more professional, it also makes you appear more trustworthy, as every email you send and receive is accountable to the company you represent.

2. **Do be concise and to the point:** Do not make an e-mail longer than it needs to be. Remember that reading an e-mail is harder than reading printed communications and a long e-mail can be very boring and can put off the reader. The place for small talk is in person, not via email. Get to the point of what you need to say or ask quickly.

3. **Do use formal language:** Emailing isn't texting, and your colleagues and clients are not your buddies. When sending a business email, always use full sentences, avoid colloquialisms like "yo" "ya" and "hey" in the greeting line, and use the recipient's full name unless they have already told you that they prefer a nickname. Even if you know a client extremely well - even if you're friends outside of business hours - using full sentences and formal language is good practice; you never know what information is going into business files or being passed on to others.

4. **Do use a relevant subject**: Use a subject that is meaningful to the recipient as well as to you. For instance, when you send an email to a colleague about preparation for an upcoming meeting, it is better to mention the actual details, e.g. 'Product A- PPT for Sales Meeting on 1st Sept' than to just say 'meeting information' or the products name in the subject.

5. **Do use active instead of passive voice:** Always use the active voice of a verb wherever possible. For instance, 'We will settle your complaint today', sounds better than 'Your complaint will be settled today'. The first sounds more personal, whereas the latter, especially when used frequently, sounds unnecessarily formal.

6. **Do keep your language gender neutral**: In this day and age, avoid using sexist language such as: 'The user should add a signature by configuring his email program'. Apart from using he/she, you can also use the neutral gender: "The user should add a signature by configuring the email program'.

7. **Do take care of the formatting:** Remember that the sender might not be able to view formatting, or might see different fonts than you had intended. So always try to use a generic font like 'Arial' that will open in any system. When using colors, use a color that is easy to read on the background, preferably black or dark blue.

8. **Do use proper structure and layout**: Since reading from a screen is more difficult than reading from paper, the structure and layout is very important for email messages. Use short sentences and paragraphs. When making points, number them or mark each point as separate to keep the overview.

9. **Do answer all questions, and pre-empt further questions**: Your email reply must answer all questions, and pre-empt further questions. If you do not answer all the questions in the original email, you will receive

keep receiving further e-mails regarding the unanswered questions. This will not only waste your time and your customer's time but also cause a lot of frustration for both of you. Going a step further, if you are able to pre-empt relevant questions, your customer will be much impressed with your efficiency and thoughtful action.

10. **Do check for spellings, grammar and punctuation**: This is very important as improper spelling, grammar and punctuation leave a poor impression of your company in the mind of the recipient. Improper punctuation such as no full stops or commas are difficult to read and at times, even changes the meaning of the matter. Finally, it is also important to convey the message properly.

11. **Do reply as quickly as possible:** From your end do your best to reply as quickly as you can, especially if you have been asked to perform a task or supply information. If you know that it is going to take some time to respond properly, then send a quick response to let the recipient know that you received the email and are working on the detailed information required. This will put the recipient's mind at rest enabling them be more patient! It is certainly considered rude and improper etiquette to keep someone waiting for a response, but it does not take very long to at least make it clear that you received the message. Ideally an email should be replied to within at least 24 hours and preferably within the same working day.

12. **Do make it personal:** All emails must be personally addressed to the recipient by name with the content of the email being customized to suit that recipient. For this reason auto replies are usually not very effective. However, templates can be used effectively for other reasons as you will see in the next point.

13. **Do use templates for frequently used responses:** There is certain type of information that you keep getting over and over again, such as bank account details, directions to your office etc. You may have a standard response to these. Create these texts in a professional format as response templates and paste these into your message when you need them. You can save your templates in a Word document, or use pre-formatted emails.

14. **Do add disclaimers to your emails**: With so much happening today on the internet, it is very important to add disclaimers to your internal and external mails, as this can protect your company from any type of liability. Your company must therefore have an email policy in place and added to every outgoing email. There is a separate chapter included on this subject. Your company is confirming that it did everything it could to prevent offensive emails.

15. **Do read every email before you hit the 'send' button**: Many people fail to do a check for any spelling or grammar mistakes contained in emails. After all it takes a few minutes, but can save a lot of

misunderstandings, embarrassment and finally your image and credibility is at stake.

16. **Do use the cc: field sparingly**: Use the cc: field with a lot of caution. Try not to use it unless the recipient in the cc: field knows why they are receiving a copy of the message. Using the cc: field can be confusing since the recipients might not know who is supposed to act on the message. In general, do not include the person in the cc: field unless you have a particular reason for wanting this person to see your response. Again, make sure that this person will know why they are receiving a copy.

17. **Do be careful with the use of Bcc**: When sending an email mailing, some people place all the email addresses in the To: field. There are three drawbacks to this practice: (1) The recipient knows that you have sent the same message to a large number of recipients, (2) Causes confusion as to who is actually to respond? (3) You are publicizing someone else's email address without their permission, which is certainly unethical. Therefore this field has to be used with much discretion (this has been covered in detail elsewhere)

18. **Do take care with rich text and HTML messages**: Be aware that when you send an email in rich text or HTML format, the sender might only be able to receive plain text emails. If this is the case, the recipient will receive your message as a .txt attachment. Most email clients today however, are able to receive HTML and rich text messages.

19. **Do keep things light:** Do not ever make jokes at your colleagues' or clients' expense, but if you can inject a little humor without offending anyone, you should. It certainly lightens the atmosphere

20. **Do practice, and ask for feedback:** Writing business emails is like any business skill: you improve by doing it. If you're mindful of your email etiquette with every email you send, and you ask for honest feedback from colleagues and clients you trust, then over time, writing clear and professional business emails will become second nature to you. Just like any other part of proper business etiquette, the more experience you have, the more naturally writing business emails will come to you.

21. **And finally...**Do unto others as you would have them do unto you!

Don'ts

1. **Do not write in CAPITALS:** IF YOU WRITE IN CAPITALS IT SEEMS AS IF YOU ARE SHOUTING. This can be highly annoying. Therefore, try not to send any email text in capitals.

2. **Do not use your business email for personal communication (and vice versa):** It is a very bad idea to use your business email for personal correspondence. When you are not able to separate the two, the chances are that the moment your business contacts and personal contacts intermingle, you increase the risk of accidentally CC'ing your boss or a client on something meant for a close friend, which can be embarrassing or

even professionally damaging. Keeping the two emails separate also helps protect client confidentiality and keeps business documents more secure, which is best both for your business as well as for your customer's peace of mind.

3. **Do not attach unnecessary files:** By sending large attachments you can annoy customers and even bring down their e-mail system. Wherever possible try to compress attachments and only send attachments that are useful and productive. Also make sure you have checked with them before sending. It would be good to have an effective virus scanner in place on your system to avoid sending your document full of viruses to your customers!

4. **Do not overuse the high priority option:** If you continue to overuse the high priority option, it will lose its function when you really need it. Moreover, even if a mail has high priority, your message will come across as slightly aggressive if you flag it as 'high priority'. So use with caution and discretion.

5. **Do not leave out the message thread:** When you reply to an email, you must include the original mail in your reply, in other words click 'Reply', instead of 'New Mail'. If you receive many emails you obviously cannot remember each individual email and its content. This means that a 'thread less email' will not provide enough information and you will have to spend a frustratingly long time to find out the context of the email in order to deal with it. Therefore, leaving the thread

might take a fraction longer in download time, but it will save the recipient much more time and frustration in looking for the related emails in their inbox!

6. **Do not overuse Reply to All:** Only use Reply to All if you really need your message to be seen by each person who received the original message.

7. **Do not use abbreviations and emoticons:** In business emails, try not to use abbreviations such as BTW (by the way), LOL (laugh out loud) and other such ones. The recipient might not be aware of the meanings of the abbreviations and in business emails these are generally not appropriate. The same goes for emoticons, such as the smiley :-). If you are not sure whether your recipient knows what it means, it is better not to use it. In fact, our advice would be to totally refrain from these in all your business emails, as it does not say well of your professionalism.

8. **Do not use heavy non-conversational language:** While it's good practice to keep your emails relatively formal, you don't have to write like a legal person in your emails. Unlike formal documents, emails give an impression of who you are as a person, which means that you should try to inject a little personality into them before you hit "send"

9. **Do not request delivery and read receipts:** This will almost always annoy your recipient before he or she has even read your message. You are actually indirectly conveying to the recipient that you do not trust them, hence you require an

acknowledgement. Besides, it usually does not work anyway since the recipient could have blocked that function, or his/her software might not support it, so what is the use of using it? If you want to know whether an email was received it is better to ask the recipient to let you know if it was received.

10. **Do not ask to recall a message:** Do you think your message would not have been received? Biggest chances are that your message has already been delivered and read. A recall request would therefore sound very immature. It is better just to send an email to say that you have made a mistake. This will look much more professional and honest than trying to recall a message.

11. **Do not be abrupt, harsh or negative:** It is certainly difficult to gauge the tone in any email, which means that sometimes, you may be coming across much harsher than you intend. So at the most you could avoid negative-sounding words like "failure", "useless", or "mistake", and if you're giving feedback, make sure you offer some encouragement along with whatever criticism you're sending. I call this the sandwich effect. If in doubt, read your email aloud to yourself before sending; you might find it worth writing a few extra words explain your situation and to make sure you are not coming across unnecessarily harsh in writing.

12. **Do not copy a message or attachment without permission**: Do not copy a message or attachment belonging to someone else

without permission of the originator. It is proper etiquette to always seek permission.

13. **Do not use email to discuss confidential information:** You will never know who at the other end will be opening your email. The thumb rule is that: If you don't want your email to be displayed on a bulletin board, don't send it. Moreover, never make any vulgar, nasty, libelous, sexist or racially discriminating comments in emails, even if they are meant to be a joke.

14. **Do not use URGENT and IMPORTANT:** Even more so than the high-priority option, you must at all times try to avoid these types of words in an email or subject line. Only use this if it is a really, really urgent or important message.

    If you put "Important- please respond" in the subject line of every email, then very soon all your recipients will realize that most of your emails are not really that important after all. It is like crying 'wolf'. As much as you may want an immediate response every time, you need to be selective as to which emails you mark as "important" in the subject line, otherwise the word gets diluted and ceases to have that real important effect. If you trust that a well-crafted subject line will get the job done most of the time, then when you include the word "important" or "urgent", the recipient will actually take note.

15. **Do not use long sentences:** Try to keep your sentences to a maximum of 15-20 words. Email is meant to be a quick medium and requires a different kind of writing than letters.

Also take care not to send emails that are too long. If a person receives an email that looks like a dissertation or thesis, chances are that they will not even attempt to read it!

16. **Do not forward libelous, defamatory, offensive, racist or obscene remarks, virus hoaxes and chain letters:** If you receive a forwarded message warning you of a new unstoppable virus that will immediately delete everything from your computer, this is most probably a hoax. By forwarding hoaxes you use valuable bandwidth and sometimes virus hoaxes contain viruses themselves.

    The same goes for chain letters. Do not forward chain letters. Since it is impossible to find out whether a chain letter is real or not, the best place for it is the 'delete' folder. We can safely say that all of them are hoaxes. Just delete the letters as soon as you receive them. Don't send or forward emails containing vulgar, libelous, defamatory, offensive, racist or obscene remarks. By sending or even just forwarding such emails, you and your company can face court cases resulting in the damage of your company's image and reputation.

17. **Do not reply to spam:** By replying to spam or by unsubscribing, you are confirming that your email address is 'live'. Confirming this will only generate even more spam. Therefore, just hit the delete button and remove them.

18. **Do not assume everything will translate:** Tone is crucial especially when you are not face to face with the other person. It is how you say or put across a message. It is

important therefore to read aloud your message a couple of times, pausing at the relevant punctuations, just to see if it conveys the right tone that you intended the other party to receive. This is especially true with jokes: just because you think something is funny when you write it, there's no guarantee it will translate well to whoever is reading it.

19. **Do not send without proof-reading:** Improper spelling and grammar will give the impression that you are careless and did not pay attention to detail. It not only says well of your company but of you too, as others begin to see you as being meticulous in whatever you do. Do not let shabby email writing be a reason for your bosses, colleagues and clients to question how well you do your job. A quick proof-read is all it takes to send an email that looks polished and professional. Proof-reading before you send will also let you spot potentially embarrassing mistakes before everyone in the company hears about them.

20. **Do not hit the 'send' button until you are sure of all of the above!**

How to Email the SMART way

✓ **S**end a prompt reply, even if it is to just acknowledge their email. This lets people know you received the information. If more details are required, and you can't get to those at that time, then simply add a specific timeframe.

✓ **M**aintain the right etiquette with best impression of your email. Remember, first impressions are lasting impressions, so do all you can to maintain proper business etiquette

✓ **A**nswer all questions. Be sure you've covered all the information before you hit send.

✓ **R**eview, review, review! Read over your email before you hit the 'send' button. Check for spelling. Did you add all attachments? Finally, how is the tone of your email? Be aware that emails can hurt other's feelings, and there is also the chance of distortion on the receiving end. Communication can be risky business, so review and revise as needed.

✓ **T**hink before you send. Some messages are better on the phone or in person. So ask yourself this question: "What is the best mode to handle this? Is this best handled with an email message, or should I be speaking directly to this person so there are no assumptions and no ambiguities?"•

Avoid Email Disaster with the 5 R's

So how do you avoid email disaster? With considered planning you can master proper business emailing by conveying the right message professionally without ruining your business reputation.

Think of these 5 R's when writing proper business emails:

Don't Rush: A hurried email is often a badly formatted, badly written email. Allow yourself enough time to properly format every email you write.

Watch for Reaction: Never shoot out an email when you're upset. Instead, wait until you have calmed down.

Avoid Rambling: Be Concise. Be to the point. Use short sentences and short paragraphs. If appropriate, make use of bulleted or numbered lists.

Review: Double-check your email for typos, grammar mistakes, and other errors. It is also a good idea to make sure all the parts of the email are included.

Response: Ideally within 24 hours

Networking Skills

What is Networking?
The action of interacting with others to exchange information, ideas, and resources and develop contacts which can be for mutual benefit

Why Network?
75% - 80% of business is obtained as a direct result of some sort of networking.
There is some truth in the old saying: "It is not what you know, but who you know."
 Networking is the key to your business success

What are the main benefits of Networking?
- ✓ Access to knowledge through contacts
- ✓ Develop contacts that can provide with support and advice
- ✓ Learn from other people
- ✓ Create collaborations
- ✓ Can create otherwise unknown chances for collaboration and new opportunities.

✓ Development of your emotional and creative intelligence though added support and advice, including the support from mentors and champions
✓ Exposure to new environments
✓ Increase your confidence

The Key Steps to Networking Successfully
The best place to network is to begin in your comfort zone
Step 1: Your Comfort Zone: Your comfort zone will be in the areas you know, namely: what you want, who and where you are
✓ Your Agenda
✓ Your Story
✓ Your Questions
✓ Your Conversations
✓ Your Connection Points
Step 2: Your Objective: Before attempting to network-online or in-person, it's important to resolve in your mind the question of why. Why are doing this? What's your agenda? What is your objective of networking? What are the likely groups that you could get into? Who do you need to talk to? Target people/organizations? What do you want to achieve or find out? Where do you hope it will lead you?
How could you contact them?
✓ Looking up their profile
✓ Networking at events
✓ Asking connections
Step 3: Make a start by joining the Networking Groups you decided on in the earlier step. One recommended way to begin networking is to join at least two organizations.   One networking group related to your target market and another of your

peers. The target market group will allow you to meet people who you would like to work with and promote your business, whereas the peer group is for gathering knowledge in your field by hanging out with others like yourself.

Step 4: Do your Preparation (This step is very important)

Write down who you need to talk to, and why you want to talk to them.

Consider also, what do you want to find out? Or where would you like this to lead?

In other words, it's important to know your purpose - and in doing so you can increase your satisfaction levels afterwards.

You must have a compelling Story: Your Elevator Speech (See more on this in another earlier chapter) How do you present yourself in different contexts? And this can often be the most difficult part of any event – how to introduce yourself to strangers.

Your goal should be something like:

1. Introduce yourself to the people in your core group – these can simply be the people near you in a lecture or virtual breakout room. Try and find a connection point. Are you a trainer helping in skills they might find useful? Did you once work with one of their collaborators, mentors or trainees? Your aim should be that they remember meeting you.

2. Ensure that people in this core group know what specialty and industry you are in. Prepare your specific 'attention-grabbing' statements to answer the questions "Who are you and what do you do?"

Preparing a "story" (Elevator Speech or if you like a "statement of purpose") in advance will greatly help you settle in and take that first networking step.

Do your Homework on the Networking Group/ Event!

Things to do BEFORE the networking meeting or event:

1. Get a list of attendees
   - ✓ Ask the host or facilitator
   - ✓ Enquire online
2. Search for attendee's websites
   - ✓ Gather information
   - ✓ Review company services
   - ✓ Look at their picture
3. Select the people you want to meet
   - ✓ Write down their names
   - ✓ Call them before the event
   - ✓ Seek them out at the event
4. Ask the host or facilitator to introduce you to 2 or 3 people
   - ✓ People who would typically be a referral source
   - ✓ People who may be a potential client
   - ✓ People who are mover's and shaker's

Think about:
- ✓ What do you want to find more out about?
- ✓ How are you going to bring these questions into conversations?

Things to bring to the meeting or event:
- ✓ Have plenty of business cards with you (at least 50)
- ✓ Place business cards in your left pocket
- ✓ Name badges (if applicable)

Things to DO at the meeting or event:
- ✓ Get there early and stay late
- ✓ Introduce yourself within 60 seconds of entering the room

Step 5: What Impression do you want to create: Your first 30 Seconds Count!

"You only get one chance to make a <u>first</u> good impression."
First Impressions
- ✓ Dress for the Occasion: 60% of people are visual communicators. This means that to 60% of the world-image is key.
- ✓ Demeanor: Business entrance should be professional and quite seamless and understated.
- ✓ Introductions: Person of higher rank receives the introduction. Use the name of higher-ranking person first.
- ✓ Handshake and Share Business Card (See more on this in another chapter)

Step 6: Working your way around in the Event
1. Meet new contacts
- ✓ Do not hang with people you know
- ✓ Meet people you want to do business with
- ✓ It is not a card gathering experience
2. Look for groups of 2 or 3 people
- ✓ Get into groups already formed
- ✓ An easy way to introduce yourself to a group is "Do you mind if I join your conversation?"
- ✓ If approaching a speaker or any other group official have something relevant to ask e.g. 'I thought X part of your paper was really interesting, in particular I wanted to ask about...'
3. Seek information first
- ✓ Get others to reveal their wants and needs
- ✓ Let others shine and feel good about themselves
- ✓ Make others believe that you are listening and are interested

- ✓ Look at the other person for approximately 60% of the time. Give plenty of eye-contact but be careful not to make them feel uncomfortable.
- ✓ When listening, nod and make encouraging sounds and gestures.
- ✓ Use the other person's name early in the conversation. This is not only seen as polite but will also reinforce the name in your mind so you are less likely to forget it!
- ✓ Smile!
- ✓ Try to ask the other person open questions (the type of questions that require more than a yes or no answer).
- ✓ Avoid contentious topics of conversation.
- ✓ Use feedback to summarize, reflect and clarify back to the other person what you think they have said. This gives opportunity for any misunderstandings to be rectified quickly.
- ✓ Talk about things that refer back to what the other person has said. Find links between common experiences.

4. Give your "elevator speech"
- ✓ Reveal how you can help them
- ✓ Briefly explain what you do and how you do it
- ✓ Build their curiosity and interest in you

5. Conversation conclusions
- ✓ If you want to do business, conclude your conversation with offers and requests
- ✓ Send follow-up materials
- ✓ Introduce them to a colleague
- ✓ Ask for a business card
- Say something like *"It seems as though it would be worth following up with a more specific discussion. Would you be open to*

meeting up after the conference?" or *"I will call you tomorrow and see if we can help each other, okay?"* If they agree to a meeting see if you can schedule it right then and there with your smart phone and ask if they have theirs.

6. If you do not want to do business, conclude your conversation:

- Do not exchange business cards
- Use *the great escape* exit: *"I have enjoyed meeting you and I look forward to seeing you again."*
- Or to make a graceful exit. *"I have to make a quick call"*, or *"I'm going to get a drink of water if you'd excuse me?"* or *"I just spotted someone else I need to speak to, lovely to meet you."* or *"I've enjoyed meeting you. I know you have others you would like to meet and so would I . . ."*

Step 7: After the Event

Take time to write notes on the back of (their) business card or by using the Contacts App on your phone.

Review notes you have made

1. Write a quick note or send an email: remind them that you met them at the event and what you spoke about.
✓ Send it soon after the event (within 24 hours)
✓ Keep it simple and friendly
2. Send an article or useful resource
✓ Relevant article, important telephone number or website
✓ Make sure it is simple and helpful
3. Send a thank-you note for suggestions, ideas, and resources resulting from your contact. Show appreciation

4. Do them a favor
  ✓ Introduce them to associates, clients and vendors
  ✓ Help them to achieve their goals
5. Send them a referral. Ask for a follow-up call
6. Send a gift
  ✓ Make it appropriate
  ✓ Always add a note
7. Keep contacts on your mailing list
  ✓ Use contact management software for tracking
  ✓ Persistence pays

Name Placement Tags or Badges

Name badges are always worn on the right hand side of your front shoulder area. Why? The reason is that as you extend your hand in greeting, the gaze of the person you are meeting can easily follow your extended arm back allowing for a natural progression for the eyes to the name tag.

Some other good tips include:

  ✓ Arrive early. Arriving before the venue is noisy and full of people lets you get accustomed to the sights and sounds of the room before they become overwhelming. You can also scope out places to retreat to if you need a moment of solitude.
  ✓ Arrive with a friend or colleague. Not knowing anyone can be uncomfortable. Walking in with a friend guarantees you will know at least one person in the room who can introduce you to others.
  ✓ Have strategies to re-energize mid-event. Give yourself a networking time limit and then

go somewhere to regroup in solitude. Or consider taking a break to peruse the display items on the shelf or elsewhere. Sometimes you just need to be seen and not heard.

Rules for Business Introductions
- ✓ Know the status and rank
- ✓ Know the first and last names
- ✓ Pronounce each person's name correctly
- ✓ Know some piece of relative information
- ✓ Knowledge of person's job
- ✓ Use formal, academic or political title before last name
- ✓ Mr., Mrs., or Ms.
- ✓ Use formal introductions for senior-ranking executives
- ✓ Repeat person's name
- ✓ Name Tags do not replace proper introductions

And Finally…Some Deadly Networking Mistakes
- ✓ Hanging around your friends
- ✓ Staying too long in one group
- ✓ Being too busy eating and drinking
- ✓ Talking nonstop
- ✓ Asking about the weather or other irrelevant topics
- ✓ Getting pushy about meeting socially
- ✓ No follow-up or follow-through

International Business Etiquette

Etiquette is heavily influenced by culture; each country and nation having their own set of rules for polite behavior. The world has more than 200 countries, with many containing multiple cultures. When dealing with an international clientele, or when conducting business in a foreign country, it's best to be aware of local etiquette guidelines. Knowing the proper business etiquette for the country of your potential client or partner is the key to success of your business transaction. By following respected and time honored business etiquette traditions, you will effectively demonstrate your own intellect and class, proving to your foreign business partners that you are worthy and deserving of their attention, respect and business.

Research and Preparation is Paramount: Preparation is the key to ensuring a positive impact: What may be good manners in one country or to one nation may not be good manners in another. Always take the time to research cross-cultural etiquette when dealing with a foreign client, or when conducting business in a foreign country. Awareness of international etiquette is important not just in face-to-face meetings but also in non face-to-face encounters such as sending gifts, conversing over the phone or communicating online. Areas you need to look at include: Religion, Dress code- what attire is appropriate, Social hierarchy, Use of titles and forms of address, Business card /Handshake exchange, Non-verbal communication -what is read between the lines, Introductions-how to get started on the right foot, Personal interactions- Topics to be discussed and not discussed, Valuing Time, Physical Space, Dealing with embarrassment, Gift exchange, How to work with an interpreter

General Tips
Here are some important points when dealing with other cultures:
- ✓ Some cultures dress conservatively as the norm. Americans tend to be more relaxed when it comes to dress codes, and even recommend dressing for comfort in certain fields and professions. People from other parts of the world are generally more conservative. The Japanese, for example, dress according to rank. Some Muslim nations find short dresses for women as offensive. If uncertain, stick to the safer side of conservatism.
- ✓ Some cultures meet and greet people with a kiss, a hug, or a bow instead of a handshake. A handshake for greeting is mostly universal. However, don't be surprised if you are occasionally met with a kiss, a hug, or a bow somewhere along the way.
- ✓ Stick to formal titles for business interactions unless invited otherwise. Approach first names with caution when dealing with people from other cultures. Some cultures are very hierarchical, and will consider it disrespect to be addressed without their title. Some cultures never accept first names in the business setting, and this should be respected.
- ✓ Some cultures are less time-conscious than others. Don't take it personally if someone from a more relaxed culture keeps you waiting

or spends more time than you normally would in meetings or over meals. Stick to the rules of punctuality, but be understanding when your contact from another country seems unconcerned.

✓ Understand differences in perception of personal space. Americans have a particular value for their own physical space and are uncomfortable when other people get in their realm. If the international visitor seems to want to be close, accept it. Backing away can send the wrong message

✓ Making eye contact: Don't be alarmed when a guest from France or Middle East locks eyes with you and gives a prolonged intense stare. This is common, in fact, the guest may move even closer to get better eye contact. The opposite is true with Britons. Each country will be slightly different in their non-verbal communication and the amount of personal space that they leave. Don't assume it is OK to touch someone.

✓ Business Cards: The degree of formality of business card etiquette varies from country to country. In general present your business card with both hands holding the top corners so recipient can read it. Also receive business cards with both hands when possible. It is considered respectful to spend time reading their card. Asians assume you will have a business card holder, so putting a card in your pocket is considered crude. Many nationalities like to have their language printed on the back to help translate the title (South America, Asia,

and Northern Europe). Do not write on their business card, as this is defacing the card
- ✓ Body Language: Not only do other cultures speak a foreign language, the body language and gestures are different too. Showing the soles of your shoes while crossing your legs is very offensive with many other cultures. A finger on the nose means "confidentially" to a Briton. Nodding the head means "no" instead of "yes" in Greece and Turkey. Thumbs up is an offensive gesture in parts of Latin America and Africa
- ✓ Accepting a drink: Alcohol is common in many of the international cultures, so be prepared to be offered a drink. Do not turn down an offer of vodka from a business associate from Russia as this is considered highly offensive
- ✓ Gifts: Gifts are given to show gratitude, including as a way to thank someone for a hospitable act. If you are the host, it is not always appropriate to give a gift. Choosing the right gift and presentation is important - wrap the gift, using red or yellow paper - avoid white or black wrappers and ribbons

Give at the end of meeting, presenting and receiving with both hands but expect polite refusal at first. Other considerations: With Chinese, the gift must be given in a group setting or it will appear to be a bribe. With Japan, the gift should be wrapped or it may be considered rude- It's all about the box. Other cultures place meaning on symbols, colors and number. For example, a clock may be considered a death gift in China. The number 4 is extremely unlucky and will be taken with offense in certain places. Do not open the gift unless you are invited to. Present your gift at the end of the meeting or agreed upon time. Be aware of the culture you are in when wrapping the gift. Always carry three levels of gifts to use as appropriate

✓ Topics to avoid: Jokes as some may not understand and they usually don't translate. Negative comments about guests' country's policies or policy makers, and religion, etc must be avoided

Here are some tips by specific country:
South East Asia
China
Being on time is vital
Use formal titles when introducing yourself. Have your business cards printed in Chinese and present business cards with both hands. Exchange business cards at the beginning of the meeting during the introductions. Include gold embossing on your card because it represents wealth, status, and prestige in Chinese cultures. Upon receiving your colleagues' business cards, read them attentively before putting them away carefully and respectfully. Putting a business card directly into your pocket without reading it is highly insulting to Chinese businesspeople. The way you treat the business cards indicates the degree to which you value your relationship with them.

Introduce and address your Chinese colleagues by title and last name, never by first name. During introductions, avoid overly strong handshakes because they are considered offensive and inappropriate for business meetings. Following the introductions, start with small talk before moving on to more serious business matters.

Avoid direct eye contact. Do not offer gifts privately, as these are considered forms of bribery. Do not physically touch your Chinese colleagues.

Where possible, suggest "I'll look into," rather than the closed option of "No."

Wear conservative, dark, simple attire. Bright colors and/or ornate designs are considered flashy and inappropriate. Use conservative suits with subtle colors; Women should avoid high heels and revealing clothing

Do not only discuss business at meals. Speak slowly and pause between your sentences when speaking during a business meeting. At the table try every dish offered

The Chinese hosts should leave the meal first

Japan

Japan has the second largest economy in the world with about 130 million people that speak Japanese world-wide making it the ninth most common language- also the third largest group of internet users.

Avoid using harsh language, refrain from being confrontational and from openly disagreeing with your Japanese colleagues. The Japanese value trustworthy business partners.

Be prepared to answer direct questions such as "How much money do you make?" or "How old are you?" These questions are not considered offensive in Japan and are a way for your Japanese colleagues getting to know you

The customary greeting is a bow. It is proper to exchange business cards at the beginning of the meeting and be sure to take time to read your colleagues' cards before putting it away carefully and respectfully. It is customary to bow slightly when handing out your card. When toasting, do not lift your glass off the table. Respect personal space. Silence is valued in Japan, so do not force conversation at dinner. Do not be surprised if your Japanese colleagues go silent and close their eyes. This is a sign they are thinking critically.

Dress indicates status; dress to impress. Men should wear dark, conservative suits. Women should not wear pants and should wear low shoes. Do not slurp your noodles to indicate you have enjoyed them. It is appropriate for women to drink at dinner if the host orders drinks for the group

Korea

Present your business card with both hands, and, as with Chinese or Japanese associates, be sure to attentively read your Korean colleague's card before putting it away. Acknowledge those with highest status first, followed by the oldest.

Wear a dark-colored conservative business suit to meetings. When in a Korean business meeting, instead of directly saying "no", show your disagreement by inhaling through closed teeth, tipping back your head, and saying "maybe". When speaking to your Korean associates be sure to pause frequently to allow for questions and deliberations.

Send proposals and meeting agendas prior to the meeting to allow your Korean colleagues some time to review them. Expect your Korean colleagues to deliberate with each other before making a decision. Some of the values respected in Korea are: Certainty and structure, Collectivity and Team Work, Conformity, Loyalty, Obedience and respect for authority

Europe
UK

Attire should be conservative- Men should wear laced shoes preferably, formal.

Avoid personal questions or staring. Eye contact is rarely maintained throughout a conversation. Respect personal space. Business lunches are often conducted in a pub.

Do not discuss work at after-hours social events. Do not toast anyone older than you

France

Businessmen and women in French-speaking countries value formality and respect in a business relationship. Dress conservatively. Exchange of business cards is most often after initial introductions. Maintain eye contact during discussions. Exaggeration is interpreted as boasting, and even rude. Do not be afraid to debate with your French colleagues. Business partners who make logical arguments and have well rounded views are valued by the French. Avoid overly friendly behavior. Do not discuss business during meals.

Germany

German is one of the most widely spoken languages in Europe and two-thirds of all international trade fairs take place in Germany. Keep in mind that German business etiquette is strict and distinct from most other European countries.

Until you are personally invited to use a colleague's first name, address him or her by surname and title. Punctuality is paramount in a German business meeting so at all costs, avoid being late. Dress conservatively with minimal accessories. Maintain eye contact when speaking and listening. Shake hands before and after a business meeting with a firm, brief handshake to everyone in the room. Formally write up decisions and meeting notes and share them with your German colleagues.

Always knock before entering a room and allow those in higher positions to enter first. When a man and woman are of equal status, the man will enter first. Also, wait to sit until being instructed. The most senior-ranking individual will most often direct you.

Avoid extending meetings past their established schedules. Avoid exaggeration and high pressure talk.

Italy

When scheduling meetings, do it well in advance, with the most appropriate manner being in writing and reconfirming the same with a call. Business meetings are a time for each party to discuss ideas and issues, but not to make decisions, so avoid high-pressure tactics and do not expect decisions to be made. Expect your Italian colleagues to be descriptive, talkative and demonstrative. Italians value personal relationships, so third-party introductions are helpful.

Wear a few elegant accessories, as this display of wealth translates to power in the business arena. It is also very important to honor all agreed-upon verbal commitments in order to maintain credibility with your Italian business colleagues. In addition to a business card, it is important to have a social card, containing name, phone number, title, and academic degree, for non-business interactions.

Spain

Spanish businessmen will prefer to do business with people they know, so they may want to get to know you better through dinner or other social engagements before a business meeting takes place. Wear conservative business suits with a few accessories to indicate status and wealth, and to increase credibility. Communicate face-to-face whenever possible.

It is important to accept their invitations to prove your willingness to do business. Also, it is preferable that you be introduced to prospective Spanish clients through a mutual acquaintance. Once a business meeting is scheduled, do not be surprised if your Spanish associates arrive 15 minutes late. As always, you should arrive on time despite your colleagues' expected lateness. During meetings, expect Spanish colleagues to stray from the agenda.

Once a personal relationship is established, your Spanish colleagues will be loyal to you, not to the company you work for. Expect your Spanish colleagues to deliberate after a meeting rather than make a decision in your presence during the meeting.

Establish an oral agreement before drawing up a formal contract

Russia

Shake hands firmly and maintain eye contact while doing business with Russians. Wear dark, conservative business suits. Women should wear knee length skirts rather than pants-suit. Russians value patience and appreciate the opportunity to debate and digest negotiations. Avoid pressuring your Russian colleagues into making decisions, as this is considered rude and unprofessional.

While your Russian associates may not be on time for meetings, they expect that foreign counterparts will be punctual, if not early. Also, do not expect an apology from a tardy Russian colleague as they consider their behavior a test of your patience.

If discussing technical issues during your meeting, bring an expert along with you. Russians expect a thorough presentation and want to fully understand the topic before making a decision. Expect Russians to display emotion by becoming angry, storming out of meetings, or threatening to terminate your business in an attempt to gain the upper hand in negotiations.

Avoid showing the soles of shoes as this is considered highly disrespectful.

Middle East-Arabic Business Etiquette

Rather than greeting with a "hello" or "good morning," greet your Arab associate with the traditional Islamic greeting "Assalamo Alaikum," which translates to "May peace be upon you and may God's blessings be with you."

When planning a meeting, keep in mind Islamic principles and culture value structure. When choosing a restaurant, respect Islamic dietary restrictions. Some of your Islamic associates may not eat meat or pork so be sure there is an abundance of vegetarian options. Refrain from smoking cigarettes, drinking alcohol and consuming caffeine during meetings.

Certain values like consistency, loyalty, and respect for authority are very much respected in Arab countries. By creating and staying with a set agenda, you will demonstrate not only your organization and business savvy, but also your knowledge of and respect for Arabic business etiquette.

Bahrain: Smiling and direct eye contacts are essential parts of proper business etiquette in

Bahrain. Don't be surprised if your Bahrain partner gives and expects a kiss on the cheek upon greeting you!

Saudi Arabia: Outsiders are subject to Saudi Islamic law, which bans alcohol, drugs, pornography and pork.

United Arab Emirates: The lobbies of large hotels are the preferred venue for business meetings in the UAE, as these rooms limit distraction and give attendants easy access to refreshments.

Part 2
Dining Skills and Table Manners

Restaurant and Dining Skills- Mastering Table Manners

What are Table Manners? Simply put, they are a set of rules that govern the expectations of social and dining behavior in a workplace, group or society and are a visible sign that you are a polished and knowledgeable professional

The question constantly arises, "Why are table etiquette and table manners so very important?"

It goes without saying, that understanding proper table etiquette and practicing good table manners are in part of what makes us civil human beings.

We all observe how other people act and we make judgments, whether positive or negative, on their behavior. Our practice of table etiquette is a reflection of our "breeding", not in the sense of genetics, but in how we have been educated and brought up.

Table manners play an important part in making a favorable impression. They are visible signals of your manners, and therefore, are essential to professional success. Whether having lunch with a prospective employer or dinner with a business associate, your manners speak volumes about you, your social skills and confidence, leaving a lasting impression-good or bad. Therefore being familiar with the rules of dining etiquette and the manners at the dining table can help to increase your professionalism in unfamiliar situations.

Most interviewees wrongly get the impression that the meal that they are invited out to is a time to relax and chat it up with the interviewer. The actual truth is that when an organization hosts a meal during an interview, they are assessing how you conduct yourself, your knowledge of etiquette and standard dining practices, and they are also observing how you will conduct yourself when meeting with clients and higher-ups in the company. Employers need to be firmly convinced that you can represent them in social settings with customers, clients' colleagues and competitors. They will be watching your dining manners. So the focus is on the interview, not the food

In the forthcoming pages you will get to learn step by step, the right ways to carry and conduct yourself professionally at any event or at the dining table enabling you gain all the confidence required and stand out in a highly positive manner.

Business Meal Etiquette-Planning and Arrival
First Impressions Matter!

Let's begin with Planning the Event

Here are a few key etiquette tips on planning a business lunch if you are the host:

- ✓ What is the occasion? Formal/Informal?
- ✓ When are you planning to have it?
- ✓ Who are you planning to call?
- ✓ What are your guests likes/ dislikes, especially on the various cuisines? Ask when extending the invitation or give the guest a choice of two or three restaurants, if you have not yet decided on the same.
- ✓ Choose a restaurant that is not very far, that is convenient for all your guests, a restaurant you know well that has a diverse menu
- ✓ Make bookings in advance-Reserve a table/ room etc- indicate preference for seating (a spot that's quiet) Tell the person taking the reservation.
- ✓ Confirm the time and place and repeat the details of the invitation later in the conversation.
- ✓ Invite your guests well in advance (See details on the invitation below)
- ✓ Although invitations have traditionally been sent through the mail, invitations these days are through emails or WhatsApp or other electronic means, followed by a phone call, are becoming more acceptable.
- ✓ Make it clear that you are the host.

- ✓ Tell your guests what to expect so as to allow your guests to prepare in advance in case they have to bring anything along.
- ✓ Reconfirm the reservation at the restaurant/hotel one or two days before the dinner has been planned.
- ✓ Reconfirm with your guest. Call on the morning of a lunch or dinner; if you've scheduled breakfast, call the day before.

Business Invitations-Content

A Business Invitation can be formal or informal, but must have the following:

The Company name and or logo,

The Names of the host/hostess,

Invitation Openings (the following are some suggested ones, depending on your company and the occasion),

- ✓ "you are cordially invited to"
- ✓ "requests the pleasure of your company at"
- ✓ "requests your presence at"
- ✓ "invites you to"
- ✓ "requests the honor of your presence."
- ✓ "cordially invites you to"

Nature of the event- State whether the event is for breakfast, lunch, or dinner, a cocktail party or some other occasion. (Mentioning this can help them plan accordingly)

What is the purpose? To celebrate a milestone, to introduce someone or a new product, to honor a retiree, or to celebrate an occasion or just another festive event

- ✓ Date and time of the event
- ✓ Place- The address of where the event will be held, ideally with a location map in case the guests have not been before.

- ✓ RSVP- the RSVP address or phone number is in the bottom left-hand corner of the invitation.
- ✓ Special instructions- On the right hand side bottom corner are any special instructions such as attire, parking instructions, landmarks of the location etc.
- ✓ Formal business invitations are based on the company culture, tradition etc, but it must eventually uphold and promote the company's image
- ✓ For a casual gathering, there may not be a need to have invitations printed. These could be on preprinted invitations, wherein you can simply fill the blanks by hand, of what, where, and when the party will be and who is hosting it.
- ✓ Some formal invitations include an RSVP notation and your phone number or contact details on the invitation.

Responding to the Invitation

- ✓ If you are one of the guests that have received an invitation, then you must respond accordingly
- ✓ You can use the address or phone number provided on the invitation or return the RSVP card that could have also been sent along with the invitation.
- ✓ However, if "Regrets only" is printed at the bottom corner of the invitation, then you would need only get back to the host if you are not be able to attend. If your host does not hear from you, you are expected to attend. If you see a "Please reply by" a given date in the invitation, be good enough to reply by that date.

✓ Remember, that it is not right to ask to bring a guest unless the invitation states "Mr. Fernandez and Guest", as food and beverages would have been placed only for the number of people invited- and thus you would be inconveniencing the host. If you don't want to go to the party or dinner without that special someone, decline the invitation. Let the host know that you'd like to get together with him at a time when your friend can accompany you, or when the associate isn't with you. If however, such a line is indicated in the invitation allowing you to bring in a guest, then you may fill in your guest's name and details required

Arriving at the Venue
Good dining etiquette and the impression you make on your business lunch partners/ companions starts when you first arrive at the restaurant.
✓ Never be late: By arriving even a few minutes late, you could leave a bad impression and send a clear message of carelessness and thoughtlessness. Be on time- no one wants to be kept waiting. If it is an unavoidable delay, try to contact the person. Keep in mind that you never know when you will encounter heavy traffic, road blocks, construction or other delays
✓ Dress appropriately. Dress according to the invitation or suggestion by the host. Check with the organizers/ host on the right dress code. If no dress code is indicated, assume business professional

- ✓ Remember to always say a "thank you" to the valet attendant as he takes your car and tip when your car is handed back to you after the event.
- ✓ When you are before the host: If you happen to arrive at the venue before the host, then the right etiquette dictates that you wait in the lobby or reception area for him/ her. It is not appropriate to move to the table and wait.
- ✓ When you are the host: If you are the host, it is appropriate for you to wait for your guest in the lobby. When some of your guests have arrived you can proceed to the table at the right reservation time, and have the maitre d' or waiter escort the other guests that follow later.
- ✓ Greetings and Introductions: When meeting someone, rise if you are seated, smile, extend your hand and repeat the other person's name in your greeting. A good handshake is important- it should be firm and held for three to four seconds (See more under handshakes covered earlier).
- ✓ These days, in most countries in the business world, it is not necessary to wait for a female to initiate the handshake. Females/males should both be ready to initiate the handshake. However, as a precaution check the respective cultures in countries/ organizations prior to the event.
- ✓ Another important act is the introducing of people in business life, yet few people know how to do it. Be sure to explain who people are and use their full names. Also do not assume that everyone wants to be called by

his or her first name - wait until you are told to use a first name (More details on Introducing in an earlier chapter)

✓ When you arrive at the table: Remain standing until the host indicates to be seated. Wait until you are invited to be seated, or after the host first sits down.

✓ As a general rule, follow the lead of the host before removing your jacket. If the host keeps theirs on, keep yours on. If it is very hot weather, it is acceptable to ask their permission to remove your jacket. This applies to both men and women. Some restaurants may require that customers keep their jackets on during meals, depending on the occasion or event.

✓ Do not place any bags, purses, sunglasses, cell phones, or briefcases on the table.

✓ Women take purses to the table, where they're kept in the lap or at the feet.

✓ Packages, big bags, umbrellas, and other items are usually checked at the reception.

✓ Sit up straight; don't lean or place your elbows on the table

✓ Place Cards: It is not appropriate and bad manners to alter your place card setting. It has been prearranged by the host.

Duties of Gentleman and Ladies- Car, Door, Coats, Escorting

✓ Getting into a car: The gentleman will walk with the lady to the door closest to where she will be sitting. She waits as he opens the door for her. Ladies, always wait for a gentleman to open the door, as he is courteous. Ladies will sit down, backside first then swing her legs into the car (knees together). She will always say "thank you" to the gentleman. Don't forget to fasten up your seat belt!

✓ Exiting from a car: Once at the destination, the gentleman will leave the car and close his door. He will walk to the lady's door and open it. He will then give her his left hand to help her out of the car. He will close her car door. He will then give her his right arm and escort her to the event they are going to attend (dinner, movie, concert, restaurant, church, or party).

✓ When entering a building: Upon reaching the main entrance door to the event, they will drop escort arms and the gentleman will open the door for the lady. If the door opens forward, towards you, the gentleman will pull the door out, hold the door open, and let the lady pass through. If the door opens away from you, the gentleman will push the door open while walking through. He will then hold the door open while the lady walks through. If the door is a revolving door and it is already in motion, the lady will go through first and then the gentleman. If the door is a revolving door but it is not moving, the gentleman will push it forward, walking through, and the lady will follow him.

✓ Getting the Coat off, once Inside: The gentleman will offer to help the lady remove her coat. He will stand behind her and place both hands firmly on the back shoulders of her coat. She will slip her arms out while he guides her. (At some top class hotels you may be required to leave the coat in a coat claim room and leave it with the person watching the coats- the gentleman accompanying the lady must ideally assist with this). Usually, he will be given a token/ ticket with a number on it. He must give this back to the coat check person in order to be given the correct coat. It is expected that, if a coat checkroom is used and there is an attendant, you leave a small tip per coat. If no coat checkroom then the gentleman will carry the lady's coat to their table and place it on the back of her chair or on a hook nearby. Upon leaving, the gentleman will get the lady's coat, open the coat with both hands, and guide her into her coat. He will then put on his own coat

✓ Gloves: Ladies, if you are wearing gloves, take them off before going to the refreshment table and place them on your chair.

Before the Meal or Event

Before being seated
- ✓ Allow yourself some time before you actually get to your seat for freshening-up with a visit to the restroom.
- ✓ Check for the setting of your ties, bows, buttons undone, zippers, a belt that is not centered, tossed hair, earring off, smudged makeup etc.
- ✓ Turn off or keep all cell phones or other devices silent
- ✓ Place items such as purses, handbags, umbrellas, keys, or personal items under the table
- ✓ When meeting someone, rise if seated
- ✓ Smile and extend your hand, repeating the other person's name in your greeting
- ✓ A firm handshake should last three to four seconds. Both men and women should be ready to initiate the handshake.
- ✓ Do not remove your jacket unless the host does. If you are uncomfortable, you may ask the host permission to remove your jacket.
- ✓ It is considered acceptable for men to assist women with their chair but it does not always happen; in upscale restaurants, wait staff may assist.

Place Seating at a Formal Dinner
Here are some key rules for formal dinners:
- ✓ In a restaurant, the guest of honor should sit in the best seat at the table.

✓ Usually that is the one with the back of the chair to the wall.
✓ Once the guest of honor's seat is determined, the host should sit to the left.
✓ Other people are then offered seats around the table.
✓ The male guest of honor sits on the hostess' right
✓ The next most important man sits on her left.
✓ The female guest of honor sits on the host's right.
✓ The second most important woman sits on the host's left.
✓ Men and women should be alternately seated.
✓ Couples should ideally be separated.
✓ For this reason, use of round tables puts everyone on an equal basis.

Seating for Formal Dinners

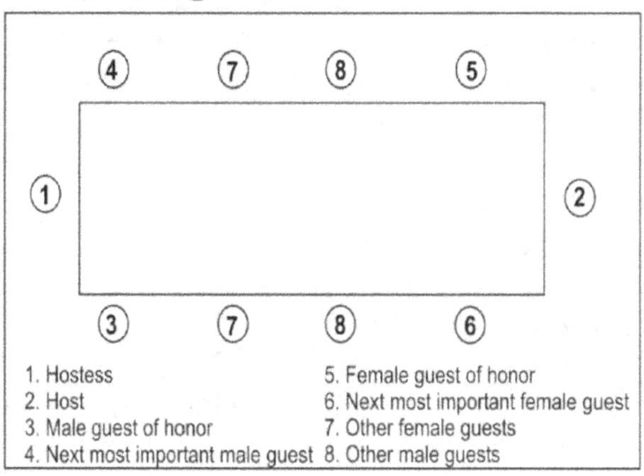

1. Hostess
2. Host
3. Male guest of honor
4. Next most important male guest
5. Female guest of honor
6. Next most important female guest
7. Other female guests
8. Other male guests

- ✓ Social manners are expected though nowadays not much practiced: males should seat females and rise when they leave and return to the table.
- ✓ There may be place cards at a formal dinner or your host/hostess may indicate where you should be seated. Your host may have seating arrangements in mind, so you should allow him to direct you to your seat. If you are the host, then you should suggest the seating arrangements.
- ✓ If in a group dining out for a meal and if there is an official host, then it's this host's responsibility to direct and guide the guests to their respective chairs. If he/she chooses not to, guests may ask where they should sit.
- ✓ At a table with a banquette, women are generally seated on the banquette along the walls, while the men on chairs opposite them.
- ✓ In earlier days, the host and hostess were usually required to sit opposite each other, and other couples split and mixed so they could have a chance to mix and converse with others. However these days, seating choices depend more on the preferences of each person and the occasion.

Posture and Poise at the Table

- ✓ Once seated at the Dinner Table, ensure that you sit up straight; do not slouch or lean over the table
- ✓ Your feet should rest flat on the floor; not crossed or wrapped around the chair legs.

✓ You may cross your ankles, but crossing legs causes slouching and makes you look too casual.
✓ Do not rock back in the chair.
✓ Keep your elbows off the table and left or right hand in your lap.
✓ Elbows on the table are only acceptable between courses when there is no plate in front of you. When you are not eating, keep your hands on your lap.

Your Posture at the Dining Table

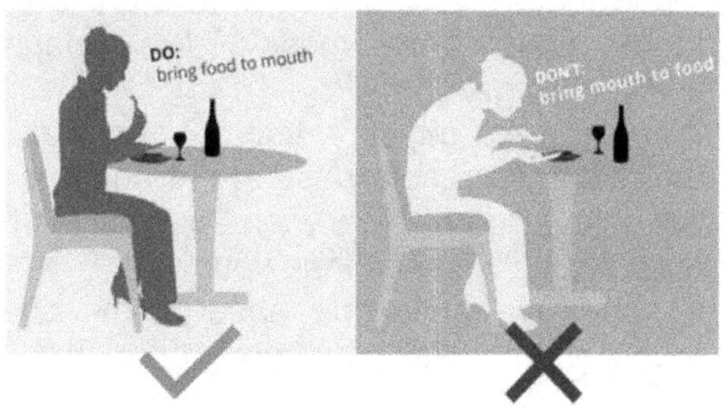

Sit up straight with your feet on the floor

When Ordering

Here are a few points to keep in mind when ordering:
✓ Once seated, take your napkin, fold it in half and place it on your lap. Again, wait staff may assist but it is appropriate to do this yourself. (See under another chapter later on the complete details of napkin etiquette)
✓ Avoid taking a lot of time to order as you could keep others waiting.

- ✓ Try not to complicate by customizing your order excessively as this can attract unnecessary and negative attention. The safest would be to follow your host's lead. Consider asking your host/hostess for a recommendation before making your decision.
- ✓ If you are the host, it is courteous to take the lead in ordering appetizers and wine, if these are to be served. Otherwise, do not order alcoholic beverages unless your host suggests or offers.
- ✓ If the host orders a bottle of wine and insists, only have ONE glass.
- ✓ Avoid foods that are difficult to eat like finger foods and/or are messy- like spaghetti, chicken wings, ribs, etc.
- ✓ If you are the guest, select an item that is in the mid-price range, easy to eat and one you will enjoy. Do not order more expensive meals or additional courses than your host.
- ✓ If you have questions about items on the menu, you can ask your server or host.

Serving
- ✓ Wait for everyone at your table to be served before beginning to eat. However, if an individual who has not been served as yet, but encourages you to begin eating, then you may do so.
- ✓ But remember to eat slowly while waiting for their food to be served
- ✓ At the Serving Table/ Buffet Service: A gentleman escorts a lady to the refreshment table. The gentleman asks the lady if she would like some refreshments. The lady may

answer, "Yes, please" or "no thank you". If the lady says yes, the gentleman picks up a plate and napkin, placing the napkin under the plate, and hands them to the lady. The lady then continues in the refreshment line and serves herself.

✓ The gentleman follows, getting his own plate and napkin and serves himself.

✓ The lady may stop at the beverage area and wait for the gentleman, who asks the lady if she would like some. Again, after the lady responds with "yes, please" or "no thank you", the gentleman picks up a cup and hands it to the lady, turning the cup so that the handle is towards the lady. A lady always expresses her appreciation. The gentleman will now pick up his own cup, and they walk back to their seats, side by side-but not in escort position. After refreshments, the gentleman may ask the lady if he may take her plate. He will carry dirty dishes to the service table. Dirty dishes are never returned to the refreshment table

Understanding the Table Setting before Beginning

Understanding the basics of table setting, can help you greatly in becoming an expert in the right dining skills. Depending upon the occasion, the placement of utensils could be "formal" or an "informal" table setting, and it's important to know how a table is set so that you could follow the proper table setting etiquette. Broadly, there are 4 Types of Table Settings:

- ✓ Basic
- ✓ Informal
- ✓ Formal
- ✓ Buffet

How utensils and tableware are placed on the table is very much like a road map that will indicate what type of a meal, the courses, and the beverages that will be served and how to go about it professionally. The right table setting for any event will depend on several factors, including: the formality of the event, how many courses to be served, and how it will be served.

So before we get into the various table settings, there are a few general table setting rules and guidelines that you must be familiar with:

- ✓ Table Cloth/ Mats: Although a formal dinner requires a tablecloth, at informal dinners a tablecloth is optional. A bare table with place mats is the alternative.
- ✓ Utensils: For starters, utensils are placed in the order in which they are used with the first ones placed on the outside. For example: the salad fork is placed on the outermost edge of

the left side before the dinner fork. This is because salads are usually served before the main course.

✓ A charger plate, also known as a service plate or under-plate, is a decorative base setting used during each dining course at weddings, banquets, or fine-dining establishments. Each course is served in a separate bowl or plate and placed on top of the charger plate. A charger plate is larger than a dinner plate but smaller than a serving platter.

✓ Forks: These are usually on the left side of the main service plate. The exception is the dessert fork which is above (top of) the plate and the oyster fork which is on the right side.

✓ Knives: Knives are always on the right side of the plate, with the cutting blade facing inwards towards the plate. The exception is the butter knife which is on the butter plate, (the butter plate is placed at the left top of the main service plate) with the blade pointing downwards and left.

✓ Spoons: Spoons are typically on the right side of the plate. The exception is the dessert spoon which is directly above (at the top of) the service plate.

✓ Placement: All utensils are usually about an inch from the edge of the table and lined up evenly from the bottom ends.

✓ Salt and Pepper: Since most people are right-handed, the salt shaker is placed to the right of the pepper shaker, in a position closer to the right hand, with the placement of the pepper shaker to the left of the salt shaker. Because salt is finer than pepper, the lid of the

salt shaker is punctured with smaller, more numerous holes than a pepper shaker.
- ✓ Only what is used depending on the event, is usually placed on the table: Eg; If there is no soup, there's no soup spoon placed.
- ✓ Coffee cups are to the right of the knife and spoon

Remember, it is never a good idea to finger around or rearrange the silverware or glassware placed in front of you

Basic Table Setting Items:

At the Center
- ✓ Service plate: The service plate, or entrée plate, is on top of the charger (if one is provided-though in most basic settings it may not), and is usually taken away before the next course.
- ✓ Napkin: The napkin is folded and on top of the plate before service begins.
- ✓ Menu card: The menu card is either on top of the napkin or inserted into the folds of the napkin for a more formal display.

At the Left-side
- ✓ Salad fork: Salad is the second course that is served, so the salad fork is at the outer left edge of the table setting. The salad fork is usually smaller than the dinner fork.
- ✓ Dinner fork: The dinner fork is to the immediate left of the charger or service plate. The dinner fork is typically the largest fork.

At the Right-side
- ✓ Soup spoon: Soup is typically the first course that is served. Therefore, the soup spoon is on the outer edge of the right side.

✓ Dinner knife: The dinner knife is to the immediate right of the service plate, corresponding with the placement of the dinner fork.

At the Top (above the service plate)
✓ Water glass: This glass is the largest of the glasses.
✓ Wine glass: A single wine glass is all that will be provided for a basic table setting, if wine is on the list for the event or function.

Informal Table Setting Items:

At the Center
✓ Service plate: The service plate, or entrée plate, is on top of the charger (if one is provided), and is usually taken away before the next course.
✓ Napkin: The napkin is folded and on top of the plate before service begins.
✓ Menu card: The menu card is either placed on top of the napkin or inserted into the folds of the napkin for a more formal display.

At the Left-side
✓ Salad fork: Salad is the second course that is served, so the salad fork is at the outer left edge of the table setting. The salad fork is usually smaller than the dinner fork.
✓ Dinner fork: The dinner fork is to the immediate left of the charger or service plate. The dinner fork is typically the largest fork.

At the Right-side
✓ Soup spoon: Soup is typically the first course that is served. Therefore, the soup spoon is on the outer edge of the right side.

- ✓ Salad knife: The salad is served after the soup, so the salad knife is to the left of the soup spoon.
- ✓ Dinner knife: The dinner knife is to the immediate right of the service plate, corresponding with the placement of the dinner fork.

At the Top (Above the Service Plate)

- ✓ Dessert teaspoon: This is above the entrée plate and is the smallest of the spoons.
- ✓ Water glass: This glass is the largest of the glasses.
- ✓ Wine glass: A single wine glass is all that you will find for an informal table setting.

The Various Table Settings

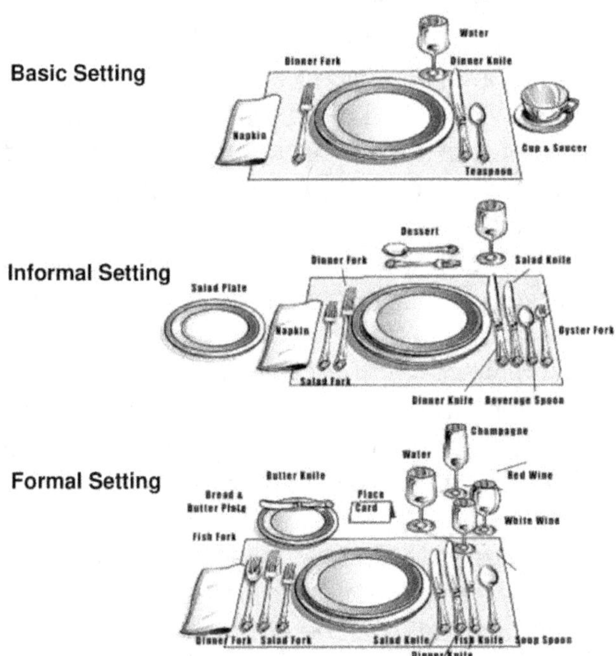

Very Formal Table Setting Items
At the Center
- ✓ Charger or Main Service Plate: The charger is the center stage of the table setting. As various courses come and go, these are set on top of the charger, including the salad course, soup course, and fish course. When the dinner course arrives, the charger is taken away.
- ✓ Service plate: The service plate, or entrée plate, is placed on top of the charger, and is usually taken away before the next course.
- ✓ Napkin: The napkin is folded and placed on top of the charger before service begins.
- ✓ Menu card: The menu card is either placed on top of the napkin or inserted into the folds of the napkin for a more formal display.

At the Left-side
- ✓ Salad fork: Salad is the second course that is served, so the salad fork is placed at the outer left edge of the table setting. The salad fork is usually smaller than the dinner fork.
- ✓ Fish fork: Next to the salad fork is the fish fork. In a formal setting, the fish or seafood course is served after the salad. Traditionally, the shape of the fish fork is designed to optimally lift the flesh away from the bones. In a dinner without a seafood course, the fish fork is used as the second course fork.
- ✓ Dinner fork: The dinner fork is placed to the immediate left of the charger or service plate. The dinner fork is usually the largest of the three forks.

At the Right-side

- ✓ Soup spoon: In a formal service, soup is the first course that is served. Therefore, the soup spoon is placed on the outer edge of the right side.
- ✓ Salad knife: The salad is served after the soup, therefore the corresponding knife is placed to the left of the soup spoon.
- ✓ Dinner knife: The dinner knife is to the immediate right of the service plate, corresponding with the placement of the dinner fork.

Above the Service Plate (Top)
- ✓ Butter plate: This plate is at the top left corner of the place setting.
- ✓ Butter knife: This is on top of the butter plate, pointing left with the blade facing down so that the handle is towards the guest.
- ✓ Dessert teaspoon: This is above the entrée plate and is the smallest of the spoons.
- ✓ Dessert fork: This is beneath the desert teaspoon, and can be used for the fruit course.
- ✓ White wine glass: The white wine glass is placed closer to the guest, as it is usually served before the red wine, along with the second course.
- ✓ Red wine glass: The red wine glass is larger and taller than the white wine glass.
- ✓ Champagne flute: The champagne flute is placed to the outer right of the glasses, because it accompanies the first toast.
- ✓ Water glass: This glass is the largest of the glasses, and is placed closest to the guest directly above the knives.

A Typical Buffet Setting

The buffet setting includes only the very essentials, and usually there will not be a plate or charger placed on the table, as the plates are usually picked up at the buffet table for the guests to serve themselves.

At the Buffet Table

- ✓ Service Plate and Napkin: Plates and Napkins are usually at the buffet table at the start of the buffet line. Sometimes each of these are just placed on each ones table in the center.
- ✓ Menu card: This is either in the form of a formal display, that spells out the items on the buffet table or alternatively, the name and description of each dish is on a label placed near the respective dish

At the Left-side

- ✓ Salad fork: Salad is the second course that may be had, so the salad fork is at the outer left edge of the table setting. The salad fork is usually smaller than the dinner fork.
- ✓ Dinner fork: The dinner fork is to the immediate left of the charger or service plate. The dinner fork is typically the largest fork.

At the Right-side

- ✓ Soup spoon: As soup is typically the first course, the soup spoon is on the outer right edge of the table setting.
- ✓ Dinner knife: The dinner knife is to the immediate right of the service plate, corresponding with the placement of the dinner fork.

At the Top

- ✓ Water glass: This glass is the largest of the glasses.

✓ Wine glass: A single wine glass is all that's needed for the buffet table setting, if it is part of the menu.

Note: Sometimes the entire cutlery mentioned above is placed on the buffet table and not on individual tables, along with the plates and napkins- in very informal settings, where each one helps themselves to whatever cutlery is required

How to work through the setting:

The best way to know how to work through the place setting, is to remember the basic rule, that all silver or glassware are arranged in the order a person will need to use them- and you must always begin from the outside. Solids are always placed to the left, while Liquids are always to the right. In order to remember the order, think BMW: Bread plate on the left, Main course in the middle, and the Water on the right. Start to use utensils on the outside first and work your way inward.

So, as an example, if you are served a salad first, use the fork set to the far left of your plate. Therefore the salad knife and fork (or the soup spoon if soup is served first) will be used first, then you will move towards the plate and continue with the main course by using your dinner knife and fork.

If dessert is ordered, you must then use your dessert fork and spoon located horizontally just above the main plate.

Your water glass is the one above the knife in your place setting and your bread plate is to the left. Sometimes the cutlery may be too close to the one seated next to you and you could be confused as to, whose bread plate or glass it belongs to. To help you through this confusion, remember "b" and "d". As you touch the index finger on your left hand to your left thumb, the "b" formed by your left hand is for "bread" (your bread plate is always to the left of your place setting). And as you touch the index finger on your right hand to your right thumb, the "d" formed by your right hand is for "drink" (your drinking glasses are always at the right of your place setting).

Remembering the Placements

The letter' **'b'** to remind of:
Bread (Solids)

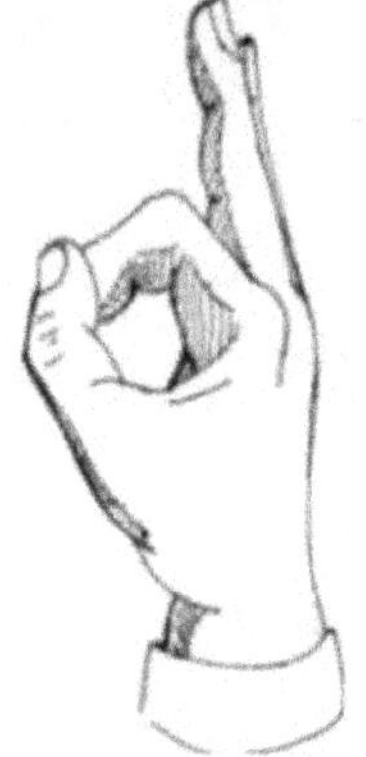

The letter' **'d'** to remind of:
Drinks

More on this in the following chapters

The Various Course Meals

Meals are divided into courses, which refers to items served together at once. For example, soup and crackers are a course; so also are a salad, dressing, and bread served together. There is usually a pause in between courses, and the parts of a meal are brought out in a specific order. For example, if you order dessert and a main dish, two examples of courses, then your entrée will arrive before the dessert unless you specify you want a different order. Full course meals are made up of three courses: an appetizer, main dish, and dessert. Also known as a three-course meal or a standard course meal, you will sometimes see restaurants offering a full menu with these three items. You can add more courses to a full course meal.

Here are some examples of the different types of full course meals with the appropriate dishes listed:

- ✓ A single-course meal includes only a main dish or entrée.
- ✓ A two-course meal serves either a soup/salad followed by an entrée or a main course and finishes with a dessert item.
- ✓ Three-course meals have an appetizer, an entrée, and dessert.
- ✓ A four-course dinner includes a soup, salad, entrée, and dessert.
- ✓ Five-course meals serve an appetizer, soup, entrée, dessert, and cheese, or Soup, Fish, Main course, Dessert and Cheese or Soup, Appetizer, Salad, Main course and Dessert
- ✓ A six-course meal offers hors-d'oeuvres, soup, fish, and an entrée, followed by salad, coffee,

and dessert or Amuse-bouche, Soup, Hors d'oeuvres, Main course, Salad, Dessert or Appetizer, Soup, Fish, Salad, Main Course, Dessert

Here is an example of a classic French eleven-course meal including typical dishes for each course in brackets:

- ✓ First course- appetizer (green salad, smoked salmon)
- ✓ Second course- soup (cream of tomato, minestrone)
- ✓ Third course- fish (salmon, trout)
- ✓ Fourth-course- entrée (steak tartare, chicken breast)
- ✓ Fifth course- meat joint (roast leg of lamb-to work with a lamb wine pairing)
- ✓ Sixth-course- sorbet (lemon sorbet, raspberry sorbet)
- ✓ Seventh-course- roast (roast chicken, roast duck)
- ✓ Eighth-course- vegetables (spinach, broccoli, asparagus)
- ✓ Ninth-course- sweets (apple slices)
- ✓ Tenth-course- savory (crab cakes, spring rolls)
- ✓ Eleventh-course- nuts (walnuts, almonds)

Important to keep in mind are the Key Rules for a Balanced Menu

- ✓ A well-balanced menu does not duplicate taste. When cheese is served as an hors d'oeuvre, it is not incorporated in a dish served at the table.
- ✓ Because sweet foods dull the appetite, fruit is not served as an appetizer. The exception is

grapefruit, which has a sharp taste that stimulates the palate.

- ✓ When a first course is served in a pastry shell, dessert with a crust is not appropriate.
- ✓ If creamed soup is served as a first course, creamed vegetables are not included in the main course.
- ✓ When sauce is served, it is presented only once.
- ✓ From light to heavy, sour to sweet, each course is designed to meet a specific taste requirement.

Proper Utensil Etiquette
Handling the Tools of the Table

Your safest means of adhering to proper etiquette at the table would be to always follow the rule of "outside-in", as this will indicate to you, as to which knife, fork, spoon or other piece of cutlery to use at the dinner table. So always start with utensils on the outside first and work your way inward with each new course that is served. However, if you are still unsure, then just follow the host/ hostess in what they do.

Holding your Silverware: There are only two correct ways to hold and two ways or styles to use your silverware. Using your knife and fork, practice the two different methods described below and determine which one is most comfortable.

- ✓ Pencil Method: Hold the utensil like you would a pencil. It should be resting between the tips of your pointer finger and middle finger with your thumb on top to hold it in place. The end of the utensil should be resting on the webbing of your hand.
- ✓ Scalpel Method: Hold the utensil like you would a surgeon's scalpel. The tines of the utensil should face downward. Your pointer finger will press on the back of the neck and the end of the handle should be touching the center of your palm. Your remaining fingers grasp the utensil to hold it in place.

American Style vs. Continental Style
American Style
- ✓ Hold your fork like a pencil, with the shank extended between your thumb and index and middle fingers.
- ✓ Your fourth and fifth fingers rest in your hand.
- ✓ For leverage, the index finger is extended along the back of the fork, as far from the tines as possible.
- ✓ Hold the knife with the handle cupped in the palm of your left hand, along with your third, fourth, and fifth fingers.
- ✓ Place your second finger on the back of the blade.
- ✓ Hold your thumb against the side of the handle.
- ✓ Cut your food.
- ✓ Then place your knife down (blade facing toward you).
- ✓ Now switch your fork to the other hand and eat with the tines facing up

The most common method used in America is this method- you will hold your fork in your left hand, cut bite size pieces with your knife in your right hand, set the knife down on your plate, and transfer the fork to your right hand and eat. This is called the Zig Zag Method or American Style.

Continental Style
- ✓ Hold your fork in your left hand, tines downward.
- ✓ Hold your knife in your right hand, an inch or two above the plate. Extend your index finger along the top of the blade.

- ✓ Use your fork to spear, cut food and lift the food to your mouth. Do not switch hands. Continue to hold both utensils while taking a bite with the tines of the fork downwards. You can use your knife as a tool to position food on your fork.

As explained in the Zig-Zag Method above, use the utensils in the same hands as explained, but use your left hand to put food into your mouth. Either way, never cut more than 1-2 bites at a time. This is also called the European Method

Important Points to Note:
The continental style prevails at all meals, formal and informal, because it is a natural, non-disruptive way to eat.

If you are a slow eater, it is best recommended that the European method be used to speed up the process. If you are a fast eater, then the American method is best recommended to slow down the process.

Resting Position-Not Finished Yet!
When you take a break during your meal- to take a sip of your beverage or to speak with someone, rest your utensils in one of the two following styles:

- ✓ American Style: To show your server that you are NOT finished eating in the American style of dining rest your knife on the top right of your plate (diagonally) with the blade of the knife facing towards you and the fork nearby (tines up).

- ✓ Continental Style: To show your server that you are NOT finished eating in the continental style of dining, place your knife and fork on your plate near the center, slightly angled in an inverted V and with the tips of the knife and fork pointing toward each other. Make sure the tines of the fork are facing DOWN towards the plate in the Continental Style.

Resting Position

Finished Eating Position

When each course is finished:

- ✓ When you have finished eating, the fork and knife must be placed parallel to each other at the 4 O'clock or 10.20 position as if your plate were a clock.
- ✓ Make sure the blade of your knife is facing towards you and the tines of the fork face up in the American Style while the tines are down in the Continental position.

Finished Position

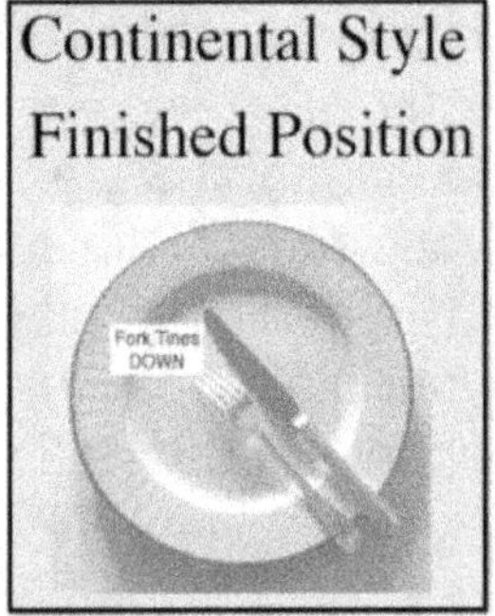

- ✓ This signals to the wait staff that you are finished.
- ✓ Always leave your dishes in place and let the wait staff remove them. Do not push plates away from you.

Other Dishes and Cutlery
- ✓ Soup spoons, coffee spoons, and dessert spoons should be placed on the service plate or saucer when you are finished eating. Never leave them in the bowl or cup.
- ✓ Never wave, or point using cutlery when you talk.
- ✓ Don't draw on the table cloth with anything, including utensils.
- ✓ Don't scrape the pattern off the plate.
- ✓ Never use your fingers to push food into your spoon or fork.
- ✓ When you are finished eating, don't push your plate away or stack your dishes.
- ✓ Never place used silverware back on the table.
- ✓ If a piece of silverware falls on the floor, do not go fishing for it. Simply push it under the table and discretely ask the server to bring you another one

Using Chopsticks
In most South East Asian countries, chopsticks are the traditional eating utensils, and knowing how to use them can add to your enjoyment of Asian cuisine. Each culture however, has their own set of table manners, though there are some general rules that will usually apply whenever you're eating with chopsticks. These are a pair of tapered sticks that are used as the primary eating utensils and are

usually made of wood, bamboo or plastic. You can also find chopsticks made out of metal, bone, and ivory. If you've never used chopsticks, at first it may seem awkward, but to start out you could practice at home using a pair of pencils if chopsticks aren't available.

Here are the steps to holding your chopsticks:

1. Hold one of the chopsticks in the groove between your thumb and fingers, by resting the chopstick on the end of your third finger (ring finger), while pressing gently with the lower part of the thumb to keep the chopstick in place.
2. Now hold the other chopstick with your thumb and first two fingers, as you would normally hold a pencil. The upper end of the chopstick rests in the groove, against the side of your first finger. The lower end rests against the end of your second finger. The tip of your first finger presses down on top of the chopstick for control, while you hold the lower end of the chopstick and your thumb steady
3. Now, using your first two fingers move the upper chopstick up and down, to grip small pieces of food between the two chopsticks. The index and middle fingers do the lifting. Use the index and middle fingers to close chopsticks over food. When moving the chopsticks, note that it is the top chopstick that should be moving, while the bottom should generally be still. If performed properly, you should be able to grasp small objects such as beans or grains of rice one at a time.

Using Chopsticks

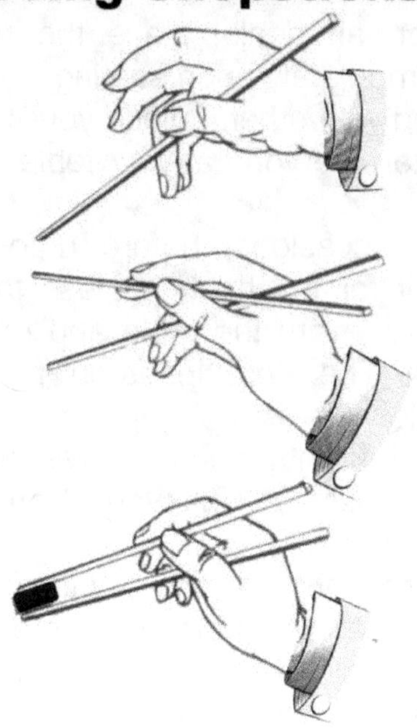

Chopsticks must always be kept in a parallel position- avoid crossing them.
Chopsticks can be used in many ways: To eat rice, dumplings, noodles, pasta, to stir soups and stews, picking up foods like meat, chicken, popcorn etc

What not to do with chopsticks
- ✓ Rest your chopsticks upright on the edge of a bowl
- ✓ Use your chopsticks to pull dishes toward you
- ✓ Pass food from chopstick to chopstick.
- ✓ Leave them stuck into a bowl of rice,
- ✓ Point your chopsticks at fellow diners

Napkin Etiquette
Here are some quick points to keep in mind about napkin etiquette:

- ✓ During informal meals, place the napkin in your lap immediately upon seating.
- ✓ When dining with others, place your napkin on your lap after everyone at your table has been seated.
- ✓ For formal occasions, before unfolding the napkin, wait for the host/ hostess to remove his/her napkin from the table and unfold it in his/her lap. The host leads in placing the napkin. Follow the lead.
- ✓ In some restaurants the waiter will place your napkin on your lap for you. You can be prepared by observation.
- ✓ Do not open your napkin in mid-air; as you remove your napkin from the table begin to open below the table level and place on your lap. The napkin should be folded and placed on your lap with the fold/ crease towards you.
- ✓ A small napkin may be opened fully. A large dinner napkin should be kept folded in half with the fold toward you. The size determines how you unfold a napkin in your lap. Large napkins are unfolded halfway, while the smaller napkins are unfolded completely and cover the lap fully.
- ✓ If a napkin ring is present, after removing your napkin, place the ring to the top-left of the setting. At the end of the meal, grasp the napkin in the center, pull it through the ring, and lay it on the table with the point facing the center of the table.
- ✓ Never tuck the napkin into your clothing, either at the waist, chin or into the collar of your shirt.
- ✓ If a napkin falls on the floor, politely ask the server to bring you another one.

- ✓ Do not wipe off cutlery or glassware with your napkin. If dishes aren't clean, ask the waiter quietly for replacements.
- ✓ Never use a napkin as a handkerchief or a bib. The napkin is used to blot your mouth, not serious wiping, and never for blowing your nose. If you must blow your nose, please excuse yourself from the table.
- ✓ For ladies, if you are concerned about your lipstick coming off on your napkin, blot it with a tissue before you come to the table. Lipstick on napkins or glasses is very unprofessional.
- ✓ If you need to excuse yourself from the table, temporarily, to go to the washroom or elsewhere leave your napkin on your chair. It is a sign to the hotel staff, that you are coming back and not to clear your table. If the chair is upholstered, place the napkin soiled side up.
- ✓ When the meal is over, loosely fold your napkin put it to the left of your place setting, and never on top of the plate. Keep your napkin in your lap until you leave the table. The host should be the first to put the napkin on the table at the conclusion of the meal. The most appropriate time to do this is as everyone is rising from the table
- ✓ If after-dinner coffee is served, then the napkin still remains on your lap.

Managing Basic to Formal Dining

Understanding a few Cutlery Rules are Key to your Success:

- ✓ Rule 1: The number of utensils indicates the number of courses. Most formal dinners will have multiple courses and typically, formal settings have seven courses: soup, fish, sorbet, a meat or fowl dish, salad, dessert and coffee.
- ✓ Rule 2: Begin with the outer utensils and work your way in. Sometimes, a utensil will be provided at the time of the specific course.
- ✓ Rule 3: Once utensils have been used, they do not lean on a plate or touch the table

Soup Etiquette

- ✓ Wait for everyone to be served, and then follow the host's lead to start.
- ✓ The soup spoon is provided by your waiter or it is on the table sitting to the right of teaspoon.
- ✓ Hold the spoon with thumb across the top of the handle, not with the handle in palm of hand.
- ✓ When eating soup, think of making a circle. Spoon away from you, bring it back around to your mouth and then back to the bowl. Dip soup spoon into soup moving away from you.
- ✓ Do not fill the entire spoon. Soup is taken from the side of the spoon so it is NOT inserted into your mouth. Sip from the edge of the spoon only- do not place the whole spoon in your mouth.

- ✓ Do not slurp or gulp or make slurping noises.
- ✓ To finish the soup, tilt the bowl away from you and use the spoon.
- ✓ When finished, rest spoon on saucer/platter. If no saucer, put the spoon on the plate under the bowl.
- ✓ Place crackers in soup only when at home alone with blinds down. Otherwise crackers should always be eaten with soup, not in soup.

Bread and Butter

- ✓ This plate is to the left of your dinner plate and above your forks. If you don't have a separate plate, it's okay to place the bread on your dinner plate.
- ✓ Bread is most often placed on the table in a basket that everyone shares.
- ✓ Because butter is produced in rectangle or square form, the butter knife is made with a dull blade to slice butter and a pointed tip to transfer cubes of butter to the plate.
- ✓ Place the bread and butter on your butter plate- yours is on your left
- ✓ Transfer butter or dips to your own plate instead of directly to the bread.
- ✓ Do not take bites directly from the roll. Tear off bite size pieces, butter them, and then eat them. Bread and rolls should never be eaten whole. Break into smaller, more manageable pieces, buttering a few bites at a time. Do not cut rolls or bread with a knife.
- ✓ Never completely cover it in butter, and do not stuff it all in your mouth at once - take small bites.

✓ Toast and garlic bread, however, may be eaten as whole pieces since they are usually already buttered.
✓ If served a hot muffin or biscuit, you may break in half crosswise, add butter, and put it back together. When ready to eat it, break it into small pieces
✓ In some restaurants, olive oil is served with bread. Dip your bite-sized pieces of bread in the oil and eat.

Passing Bread to Others
✓ If the bread is placed in front of you, feel free to pick up the basket and offer it to the person on your right.
✓ If the loaf is not cut, cut a few pieces, offer them to the person to your left, and then pass the basket to your right.
✓ Do not touch the loaf with your fingers- instead use the cloth in the bread basket as a buffer to steady the bread as you slice it.
✓ Don't hold your bread in one hand and a drink in the other
✓ Don't take the last piece of bread without first offering it to others.
✓ If a loaf of bread is served, the person the loaf is sitting in front of should cover the loaf with a clean napkin before cutting and pass the loaf to the right.

Seasonings and Sweeteners
✓ Always taste your food first before using any seasonings. Do not assume it needs to be seasoned.

- ✓ Do not be excessive with sugar or sweetener packets. The rule of thumb is no more than two packets per meal.
- ✓ Do not crumble the packets but partially tear off a corner, empty the contents and place to the side

Salads

- ✓ The salad plate is either to the left of your napkin or on top of your dinner plate.
- ✓ The salad plate is typically smaller than the dinner plate, but larger than the bread plate.
- ✓ It is perfectly acceptable to cut your salad. Ideally, the salad will be prepared so that it consists of bite-size pieces. If not, use your salad fork to cut them into smaller pieces. And if that does not work, you may use your dinner knife.
- ✓ Cut lettuce with your knife if necessary.
- ✓ Be careful with the cherry tomato, pierce it gently and cut it before placing in your mouth
- ✓ Make sure to keep your dinner knife for the main course.
- ✓ If an item falls of the plate, pick it up with a utensil and place it on the edge of the plate- do not eat it.

Sorbet

- ✓ Sorbet may be served immediately before the main course. This serves as a palate cleanser, so that you can appreciate the flavors of the main entrée.

How best to enjoy various food items-Fingers, Fork, or Spoon

- ✓ Artichoke: Use fingers to pull each leaf to dip in butter
- ✓ Asparagus: Fingers
- ✓ Bananas: Fingers
- ✓ Berries, melons, and grapefruit: Spoon
- ✓ Brownies and cookies: Fingers
- ✓ Cake: Can be broken and eaten like bread or crackers, or it may be eaten with a Fork.
- ✓ Celery, Carrot Sticks: Fingers
- ✓ Celery, olives, radishes, salted nuts, bonbons, preserved ginger and other trifles: Fingers
- ✓ Cheeses (Soft): Fork
- ✓ Cheese Cubes: Fingers
- ✓ Chips: Fingers
- ✓ Corn on the Cob: Fingers
- ✓ Crispy bacon: Fingers
- ✓ Cut fruit in a plate: Fork
- ✓ Dinner Rolls: Fingers
- ✓ French Fries (at the dining room): Fork
- ✓ French Fries (fast-food, picnic): Fingers
- ✓ Fried Chicken (dining room): Fork
- ✓ Fried Chicken (picnic): Fingers
- ✓ Grapes, plums, cherries, apples, peaches and other whole fruit: Fingers
- ✓ Ices, stiffly preserved fruits, etc: Fork.
- ✓ Lump sugar: Fingers, if no tongs provided
- ✓ Onion rings: Fingers
- ✓ Pizza: Fingers
- ✓ Potato: Use the Fork to break up a potato on your plate; do not use the knife.
- ✓ Sandwiches, Hot Dogs and Hamburgers: Fingers
- ✓ Spaghetti: Fork and Spoon

- ✓ Strawberries or dessert: Fork
- ✓ Sushi: Japanese eat with Fingers –so it's best to follow that way!
- ✓ Tacos: Fingers
- ✓ Watermelon: Fork

Twirling and Eating Noodles:
Hold the fork in your right hand (for a right handed person) as if you are going to poke the noodles. Take a small amount of noodles on the fork (less than you think you will need) and raise it out of the bowl to separate it from the rest of the noodles. Put the tines of the fork at an edge of the plate or bowl that is free of food. Point the tines of the fork straight down toward the plate. Then twirl the fork to wrap the noodles around the tines. When the noodles are wrapped all around, quickly pick up the fork with the rolled noodles around it and place it in your mouth.

Some key points to remember:
- ✓ When you pick up your food to take a bite, place the remainder back on your plate while you chew. Don't hold onto it and wave around during conversation.
- ✓ Keep your napkin ready, for wiping your hands, fingers, and blotting your mouth often.
- ✓ When using sauces, place an appropriate amount on your plate in which to dip your food. This helps eliminate double-dipping into the serving dish.
- ✓ When enjoying a burger, always cut it in quarters if it's very thick.

As You Start Eating, you must keep these points in mind

- ✓ If it is a small table of only two to four people, then you will need to wait until everyone else has been served before starting to eat. At a formal or business meal, you should either wait until everyone is served to start or begin when the host asks you to. You may begin eating when the host/hostess picks up their utensils.
- ✓ Remember that business meals are not about the food- they are about business first.
- ✓ Take small bites and never speak with food in your mouth- always finish chewing before speaking. Close your mouth while eating and never make noises when you eat. If a question is asked of you mid-bite, take a moment to chew and swallow your food. It is better to speak after a few seconds than to immediately blurt out your answer with a mouth full of food. Pace your eating. Pay attention to how fast or slow the other diners are eating so you do not finish way ahead of them or lag behind.
- ✓ If a piece of food happens to slip off your plate, discreetly place it back on the corner of your plate. If it is a small piece of food or salad, leave it where it is.
- ✓ If you get a piece of an inedible item, such as a stem or bone, politely remove it from your mouth with a utensil and place it on the edge of your plate trying to cover with another piece of food.
- ✓ If encountering something un-chewable or undesirable, hold your napkin up to your mouth and discreetly dispose of it. Place your

napkin on the side and quietly ask your waiter for a new one. An alternative is to politely excuse yourself to the restroom while keeping it in your mouth, and dispose of it there.
- ✓ Toothpicks should be used discreetly and in private; not at the table. A good idea is to go to the restroom after dining to check your teeth and freshen up.
- ✓ Never season your food before trying it. Do not complain about the quality of your food or small errors. If you dislike an item in the meal, move food around on the plate a little to appear as though you at least tried it. If you have a food allergy, it is your (the guest's) responsibility to notify the host ahead of time.
- ✓ When sharing a plate of chips or veggies with a dip or sauce with others, apply the "Single Dip Rule" - that is, dip only once; do not insert a food item you have taken a bite from back into a shared bowl of dip or sauce
- ✓ Do not spit into your napkin. Do not blow on your food. If food is too hot to eat, let it sit until it cools.
- ✓ If someone decides to claim your bread plate, let it go. It is NEVER good manners to point out someone else's lack of manners.
- ✓ Do not use lipstick, makeup, floss, combs, or toothpicks at the table.
- ✓ Do not push plates away or stack empty plates when finished.
- ✓ Never ask for a doggy bag.
- ✓ Be polite to serving staff, make eye contact and say "excuse me" to get their attention as needed, and "please and thank you"

✓ When you are at a meal interview, you may feel pressured to talk so much you don't get a chance to eat your food. You should not solve this problem by talking with your mouth full. Instead, come to the interview armed with some questions to ask the interviewer. This will allow you to eat while listening to their answers and also shows that you have done your homework!

Passing Food Etiquette

✓ Plates are served on the left and removed from your right.

✓ Do not reach across the table for an item, but politely ask the person next to you to pass. Pass "community food" such as the breadbasket, salt and pepper, and salad dressing to the right- the point being that the food is to be moving in only one direction.

✓ The person closest to the plate should offer to the person on the left, serve themselves, and then pass the food to the right.

✓ Do not serve yourself first when asked to pass something. Always pass to the right, and always include the service plate. It is considered rude to use it first before passing it to the person who asked for it.

✓ When passing items such as a creamer, syrup pitcher, or gravy boat, always pass it with the handle pointing toward the recipient.

✓ Set any passed item directly on the table instead of passing hand-to-hand. Once using or taking from a passed item, set it in a "central" location easily accessible by others if possible -do not keep it close to you.

- ✓ Never use your own utensils to serve food out of a communal dish.
- ✓ One diner either holds the dish as the next diner takes some food, or he hands it to the person, who then serves himself.
- ✓ If a platter for sharing is present it is passed around the table, with each diner holding it as the person next to him serves himself, using only the serving utensils provided.
- ✓ Any heavy or awkward dishes are put on the table with each pass.

Bread Passing Etiquette (More on this covered in previous chapter too)

- ✓ If the loaf is not cut, cut a few pieces, offer them to the person to your left, and then pass the basket to your right.
- ✓ Do not touch the loaf with your fingers- instead use the cloth in the bread basket as a buffer to steady the bread as you slice it.
- ✓ Place the bread and butter on your butter plate- yours being on your left- then break off a bite sized piece of bread, put a little butter on it, and eat it.

Salt and Pepper Etiquette

- ✓ Always taste before salting. Be sure to taste the food before putting salt or pepper on it.
- ✓ Always pass salt and pepper together. If a person asks for just one, pass both anyway.
- ✓ Saltcellars. Some hosts prefer to use saltcellars, which salt shakers have largely replaced. If there is no spoon in the saltcellar, use the tip of a clean knife to take some salt. If the saltcellar is for you alone, you may either

use the tip of your knife or you may take a pinch with your fingers. If it is to be shared with others, never use your fingers or a knife that is not clean.

✓ Salt you have taken from the cellar should be put on the bread-and-butter plate or on the rim of whatever plate is before you.

A Quick-At-Glance Table Manners-Do's and Don'ts

Before you commence your Meal

- ✓ Eat something an hour before the meal, if possible, to maintain focus on the conversation, and not the food.
- ✓ If you have allergies or food restrictions and if you know in advance the restaurant where you will be dining, look up the menu and make a list of possible foods that will not hinder your allergy or dietary restrictions.
- ✓ If you are the host, you should always try to arrive at the restaurant before your guests. You may wait for your guests in the foyer of the restaurant or at your table, but if you choose to wait at your table, give the maitre d' a description of your guests and ask him to direct them to your table.
- ✓ When approaching the table in a restaurant, if the maitre d' leads the group to the table, the guests should follow the maitre d' and the host should follow the guests. If the maitre d' does not lead the group, the host should lead.
- ✓ If you are the host, and if there is a guest that is late, rather than delay dinner for everyone to accommodate the arrival of the late guest, dinner is held no longer than 15 to 20 minutes.
- ✓ If one or more guests are ten minutes late, ask the maitre d' to seat the group and show the other guests to the table upon their arrival. Once seated, the punctual guests can

order drinks and examine the menu. After waiting 15 or 20 minutes, the group should order their meals.

✓ At an informal dinner, the guests enter the dining room in whatever order is convenient. When seating arrangements are not designated by place cards, usually the hostess enters the dining room first to tell everyone where to sit.

✓ When the guest of honor is a high-ranking female dignitary, such as the President of a country, she enters the dining room first with the host. The dignitary's husband follows with the hostess. If the guest of honor is a high-ranking male dignitary, he enters the dining room first with the hostess. The host enters the dining room second with the dignitary's wife.

✓ Place cards identify the places people are to sit; they are used to eliminate confusion when more than six people dine together. At formal affairs, which usually involve a large group, individual places are always designated by place cards.

✓ Your cell phone or other personal electronics should not be part of the dining experience. Either keep on silent your personal devises or power them off for the duration of the event and keep them put away. Checking your phone at the table implies that you have something more important going on than conversing with or listening to your hosts and is considered rude

✓ The place of honor is to the right side of the host because most people are right-handed.

- ✓ Smoking of cigarettes must never happen at the table. Smoking is offensive to nonsmokers and affects the palate.
- ✓ Always follow your host's lead: when to sit, how much to order, how fast/slow to eat, what to discuss, and if/when to take off a suit jacket.
- ✓ It is not proper table manners to keep a hat on when eating. However, wearing any type hat is becoming more acceptable in fast food restaurants and in casual settings.
- ✓ As a guest, if you know a maid or a butler, rather than draw attention to the fact and interrupt conversation, give a brief greeting, such as "Nice to see you."
- ✓ If at a job interview, follow the host's lead when ordering food or drink and avoid sloppy or difficult-to-eat dishes. Do not participate in unpleasant or controversial topics of conversation.
- ✓ Seeing the room layout gives you a clue on how to proceed at the reception. If no tables are available, you should only have a drink or your food in your hand - never both.
- ✓ You should be prepared to greet and shake hands with individuals. If having a drink hold it in your left hand to keep your right hand dry and ready to shake hands. If eating hold your plate on the right hand and eat with the left hand. When someone approaches, you are able to switch the plate to your left hand and your right hand is clean and ready to shake.
- ✓ Always be ready to stand and greet people. Networking and/or mingling are an important aspect of a business function, even if the event is described as a social gathering.

- ✓ Be sure to greet or introduce yourself to the host/hostess.
- ✓ Focus eye contact on that individual and after sometime, politely excuse yourself to move on to someone else.

During the Meal
- ✓ Be generous with "please," "thank you," and "excuse me," especially with the wait staff
- ✓ Turn off or silence all electronic devices before entering the restaurant. If you forgot to turn off your cell phone, and it rings, immediately turn it off. Do not answer the call. Do not text and do not browse the net at the table. It is bad manners
- ✓ A purse on the table crowds and disturbs the setting of the table; therefore in a restaurant or public place, it is held on the lap or placed close at hand. But in a private residence it is left wherever the hostess suggests, such as in a bedroom or on a chair.
- ✓ At a banquet, eating commences as soon as those on either side of you are served. However, at a meal served buffet style, begin eating when you are ready.
- ✓ At a restaurant buffet, never go back to the buffet for a refill with a dirty plate. Leave it for the waitperson to pick up and start afresh with a clean plate.
- ✓ At some top posh restaurants, steamed hand towels are brought to diners at the end of the meal. Use the towel to wipe your hands and, if necessary, the area around your mouth. (Wiping the back of your neck or behind your ears is best not done in a restaurant.) Most

waiters will take the towel away as soon as you've finished. If not, leave the towel at the left of your plate, on top of your loosely folded napkin.

- ✓ Place your napkin in your lap immediately upon sitting down. Unfold it while it is in your lap.
- ✓ Do not hunch your shoulders over your plate. Likewise, slouching back in your chair may indicate that you are not interested in the meal
- ✓ To show you are ready to order, close your menu and place it on the table.
- ✓ Order appetizers, dessert and alcohol only if your host suggests (Limit to one alcoholic beverage to stay sharp)
- ✓ Don't order the most expensive items on the menu. If you aren't sure which price range to adhere to, follow the lead of the host.
- ✓ Avoid messy foods, such as spaghetti and ribs. It is best not to order finger foods or anything with bones
- ✓ Do not change your order once it is made, and never send the food back.
- ✓ Use the "outside-in" rule to guide you into which knife, fork, or spoon to use at the dinner table. Use utensils on the outside first and work your way in with each new course.
- ✓ The "no elbows on the table" rule applies only when you are actually eating. When no utensils are being used, putting your elbows on the table is ok.
- ✓ A cocktail glass is not brought to the dinner table because water and several wines are served with a multi-course meal. Leave the

cocktail glass in the room where cocktails are taken.

✓ Go for simple foods, such as meat, simple salad, and soup. Avoid spaghetti, pizza, and hand-held items. If it is a fixed menu, and you do not like what you are being served, remain gracious and do not refuse the food.

✓ If your dish is not what you ordered, or if it isn't cooked to order, or it tastes spoiled, or if you discover a hair or a pest in the dish, then sending the dish back is entirely appropriate. But you should discreetly inform the waiter of the situation and ask for a replacement.

✓ If you are served food that you cannot eat, eat what you can and leave the rest on your plate.

✓ If you are unfamiliar about how to eat a particular food item, you can do any of these: (1) Wait until the host starts to eat and follow suit. (2) You can ask how the food should be eaten (fingers or fork, for example). (3) You can avoid the food altogether.

✓ When asked to pass the salt, pass both the salt and pepper.

✓ Never add any seasoning to your food, without you first tasting your food. It is bad manners

✓ At a restaurant, the waiter serves food from your left and beverages from your right side.

✓ As the waiter offers you a platter, help yourself with the serving fork in your left hand and the serving spoon in your right.

✓ If soup is too hot, stir it, don't blow.

✓ When eating soup, always, spoon the soup away from you towards the center of the soup bowl.

- ✓ Crackers are not to be put in your soup during a formal meal.
- ✓ Start the bread by offering it to the left before helping yourself. Then pass it to the right.
- ✓ When holding a utensil, rest your other hand in your lap. When not holding any utensils, both hands remain in the lap. Do not fidget, and always keep your hands away from your hair.
- ✓ Food served on a plate is eaten with a fork, and food served in a bowl is taken with a spoon. When two eating utensils or two serving utensils are presented together, such as a fork and spoon, the fork is used to steady the portion, and the spoon to cut and convey the bite to the mouth.
- ✓ When a platter contains a combination of foods, take a moderate serving of each, including the garnish. If a course is presented that contains another food underneath, such as toast or lettuce, take the entire portion. As a courtesy to the last guest, make sure to leave enough food on the platter so he or she has a choice from several portions. Take the portion nearest to you.
- ✓ When served a half chicken, use your knife and fork to cut the wing and leg away from the breast before you start eating any of the meat.
- ✓ It is acceptable to eat your chicken with your fingers on three occasions: a picnic, at home, or if it is served in a basket.
- ✓ In a restaurant, if a soiled utensil is laid on the table, ask the waiter for a clean one. But in a private residence, rather than embarrass the

hostess by wiping a soiled utensil clean, bear up in silence.

✓ At an informal meal, the guests assist with service by passing the dishes nearest to them. To avoid congestion, food is passed to the right.

✓ For items on the table that are out of your reach, don't lean past the person sitting next to you

✓ When a serving bowl is passed upon request, say "Thank you." But when you have to refuse a service, a verbal rejection of "No, thank you," is provided.

✓ Cut your food into only one or two bite-sized pieces at a time. Do not cut all your meat at once; this is reserved for children only.

✓ When finger food is taken from a tray, place it on a plate. Don't lick your fingers; use a napkin.

✓ Do not speak while eating. Finish what is in your mouth, rest your fork on your plate and then speak.

✓ To prevent traces of food from your appearing on the rim of the vessel, like a drinking water glass, make sure the mouth is free of food and blot the lips with a napkin before taking a sip of a beverage.

✓ When tasting another person's food, you can either hand your fork to the person, who can spear a bite-sized piece from their plate and hand the fork back to you, or (if the person is sitting close by) hold your plate toward the person so that he/she can put a small portion on the edge.

- ✓ Always do one thing at a time at the table. If you want to sip your wine, temporarily rest your fork or knife on the plate, and then get into sipping.
- ✓ If you spill food, discreetly retrieve it with your knife or fork and place it at the side of your plate. You may also discreetly dip your napkin into your water glass and wipe a small spill from your clothing. If food falls on the floor, leave it. If it falls on the table and is a big piece, use your fork and move it to a corner of your plate
- ✓ Never leave your spoon in your cup, soup bowl, or stemmed glass. Rest the spoon on the saucer or soup plate between bites or when finished.
- ✓ Always, eat slowly, by enjoying it, as this also encourages conversation
- ✓ Eating and making a noise, like scraping a plate, loudly chewing, smacking and slurping food can be unpleasant and impolite and are bad table manners.
- ✓ Food caught between the teeth can be annoying or uncomfortable, so wait to remove it in private.
- ✓ White wine glasses are held by the stem, not the bowl. Red wine glasses may be held by the bowl.
- ✓ Asking for a second helping is not proper table manners at a formal dinner but is permissible at an informal one.
- ✓ Never hold your glass up for a refill.
- ✓ Food is removed from the mouth in the manner in which it was put into the mouth.

Food put into the mouth with a utensil is removed with a utensil.

✓ You can take up extra gravy or sauce only with a piece of bread on the end of a fork; the soaked bread is then brought to the mouth with the fork.

✓ You may not use a toothpick in public to dislodge debris from in between your teeth - not at the table, not on your way out of the restaurant; hanging the toothpick out of your mouth…only at home when you are alone in total darkness

✓ If you notice a speck of food on someone's face, you're doing them a favor by subtly calling attention to it. You might signal silently by using your index finger to lightly tap whatever part of the face is affected.

✓ If you drop a utensil, pick it up yourself if you can and let the waiter know you need a new one. If you cannot reach it, inform the waiter and ask for a replacement.

✓ If sugar, crackers, cream, or other accompaniments to meals are served with paper wrappers or in plastic or cardboard containers, the wrappers should be crumpled up tightly and either tucked under the rim of your plate or placed on the edge of the saucer or butter plate.

✓ If food is spilled on another guest, apologize and offer to pay for cleaning (but let the other person wipe up the soiled garment).

✓ Never gesture with a knife or fork in your hands.

✓ The water is for sipping, not for washing down your food. So do not gargle at the table.

✓ When sneezing or coughing at the table is unavoidable, cover your nose or mouth with a napkin and proceed as quietly as possible. Turn your head away from the table and cover your mouth. Don't clear your throat loudly. Except in an emergency, don't use a napkin to blow your nose. Leave the table and use a handkerchief instead.

✓ When a burp is coming out, cover the mouth with a napkin, quietly burp, and say, "Excuse me." For an attack of hiccups, excuse yourself from the table until they have passed.

✓ When using a finger bowl, dip your fingers into the water and then dry them with your napkin.

✓ Chewing ice at the table or spitting it back in the glass is not acceptable adult business behavior.

✓ When coffee or tea is placed on the table without first having been poured by the waiter, the person nearest the pot should offer to pour, filling his or her own cup last.

✓ If you do not wish to drink coffee or tea, simply leave your cup turned down

✓ When leaving for the restroom, simply say "excuse me, please; I'll be right back" Leaving without a word is rude.

✓ As a guest, a compliment on the cuisine is always appreciated.

✓ Don't photograph your food.

After the Meal

✓ The host will signal the end of the meal by placing his/her napkin on the table.

✓ If you are the host, inform in advance, the waiter or maitre d' that you are to receive the bill. Once the meal is finished, ask the waiter for the bill. If there is no established host at a business lunch or dinner, the most senior professional is generally responsible for the bill.

✓ Put used tissue/napkin in your pocket or purse - don't leave it on the table for others to be forced to view, or in your chair for a server to remove.
✓ It is acceptable table manners to take leftover food home from a restaurant, except if on a date or business lunch or dinner.
✓ Remember to thank your host. A thank you note is recommended!

Dining Conversations

You have very little time to make a good first impression. We had seen in an earlier chapter on how to handle that first 30 seconds, the social ritual part- shaking hands and introducing yourself. Now you must build on that first impression- you have to make that person feel good about being with you, even for a brief encounter.

According to studies, 75% of us feel awkward and shy when we meet new people and find it difficult to start a conversation with a stranger. People are afraid of being rejected, or saying the wrong thing or just not fitting into the group.

Here are a few thoughts for ensuring the right conversations at Lunches/ Dinners

- ✓ Reflect on why you are there. Consider the purpose/context of the dining experience. Is it part of a job interview process? A formal or informal gathering of co-workers? A business deal? A major project or sale? A partnership deal?
- ✓ Come prepared accordingly: Remember that business dining is all about conversation. So come prepared with appropriate dinner conversation. You need to contribute to your table talk in a way that sets other dinner guests at ease. So do all your research in advance. Who will be attending? What interests might they have? What topics are in line with the focus of the function? When the inevitable lapse in conversation occurs, know leading questions that will encourage table

guests to begin talking about themselves. Questions or statements such as: "I'm interested in knowing a little about the kind of work you do." "Please tell me about your interest in the organization represented here." "Have you heard the speaker before?"

✓ Be well informed
- What are the current events for today? Do you have small talk options ready for the function, if needed?
- Read at least one daily newspaper and a weekly news magazine
- Before going to an event, read the headlines of the day. Current events are perfect for small talk. And don't forget the sports and arts pages.
- Bring up these topics during the first conversational lull; the other person will be grateful for your filling the silence and will most likely follow your lead.
✓ Be Curious: It's not about you. Try focusing more on the other person.
✓ Wait for the host to initiate a discussion: Generally, the host initiates the business discussion. Business, if not urgent, is often discussed toward the end of the meal or over coffee. If you are the host, it's your job to steer the conversation, to suggest topics for discussion, and to make sure that everyone at the table is given the opportunity to be part of the general conversation. When the table isn't involved in a general discussion, be a good conversationalist with the people seated on either side of you.

- ✓ Pay attention to the thread of conversation and participate when appropriate. Don't interrupt or repeatedly turn the topic of conversation to you or your interests.
- ✓ Take a glance at the person to see if there is anything about them that could start a conversation. People will be flattered by and appreciate your interest in them.
- ✓ If you're at a concert, trade meet- talk about the group, the room, food, entertainment. The same goes for wherever you may be.
- ✓ Try to choose universal topics of conversation in which all may have an interest. If you can't think of anything to say, then just listen attentively, and ask questions to generate conversation.
- ✓ Ask them appropriate, relevant questions about themselves-to start the conversation. Listen actively and show appreciation as they speak. Your conversation partner feels important when you ask questions; people like to talk about themselves, so let them do it.
- ✓ When you ask questions, there is a lot less pressure for your partner- you are perceived as caring, open and humble. Be a good listener! Ask OPEN ENDED questions that lead to longer answers. These types of questions usually ask who, what, when, where, why, and how, and use verbs that deal with your senses. (Covered separately under a different chapter)

What do you think of…?

How do you know so and so…?

What got you into…?

What gave you the idea…?

Describe….tell me about.
It's a good idea to prepare some questions before you go to an event. That way you'll have something to fall back on.
- ✓ Now share brief, reflective relevant comments about yourself if asked.
- ✓ Have only one conversation at a time
- ✓ Don't dominate the table. Give everyone a fair share to speak. And remember that you are responsible for conversing with your "triangle."

Conversing with your "Triangle"

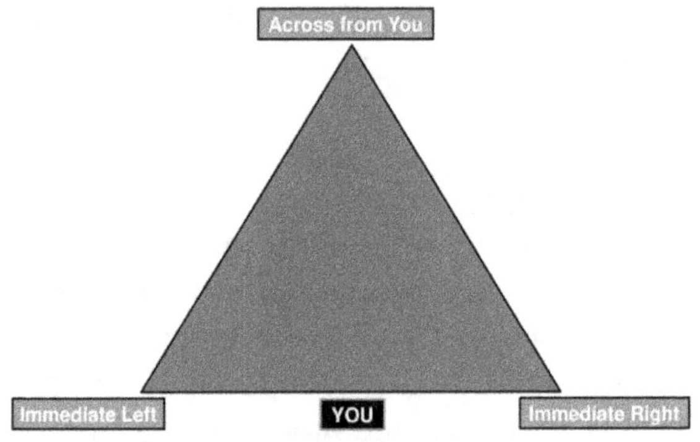

- ✓ Pay attention to people's physical needs. Do they need another drink? Something more on their plate?
- ✓ Avoid a loud tone of voice. Do not use profanities. Be sensitive to others before initiating conversation on topics that may not be suitable- avoid anything of a vulgar, graphic, or otherwise unpleasant nature. Ensure the conversation is entirely free of controversial subjects-Never tell jokes, as you never know who you could offend.

✓ If you are someone else's guest, even if part of a group, don't criticize the food, restaurant, etc. - this can cause embarrassment on the part of the "host."

Starting a conversation

A good place to start is to think of common interests. For starting a conversation or breaking the ice with strangers, think of: F.O.R.M.

F-Family

O-Occupation

R-Recreation

M-Money (economy)

Small talk can be a real saver in many situations. It fills the voids in conversations, helps ease tense moments, sets others at ease, and helps one become acquainted with others. There are two ways to make initiating small talk a little easier.

✓ The first is to be well-informed. To be able to discuss topics such as current best-selling books, news events, famous people, fitness crazes, technological advances, travel, and sports. These are all appropriate small talk subjects.

✓ The second way to ease into small talk is by asking others about themselves, their family, work, or hobby.

Here are some topics that are appropriate to speak up and get you started:

Small Talk Topics

✓ Your location or venue

✓ Shows, movies, plays, etc

✓ Art

✓ Food, restaurants, or cooking

✓ Their hobbies

- ✓ Their professional interests and responsibilities
- ✓ Sports
- ✓ The climate
- ✓ Travel
- ✓ Their local shopping favorites

Good Topics

- ✓ Current events, news etc
- ✓ Emerging Trends, Best Practices (Eg. How's business been amidst recession/ challenge etc?)
- ✓ Career Journeys + Performance/Burn Out Advice
- ✓ Food
- ✓ Memberships
- ✓ Mutual friends
- ✓ Hobbies
- ✓ Industry talk
- ✓ Styles/ Trends
- ✓ Sports

Bad Topics

- ✓ Any personal issues such as: family, health/ illnesses/ divorces/ separation/ affairs etc which may trigger something
- ✓ Religion/ religious beliefs
- ✓ Politics
- ✓ Salaries/ financial situation
- ✓ The cost of things
- ✓ Off color jokes- Racial, ethnic, and sexually oriented jokes
- ✓ Gossip
- ✓ Weight, height, shoe size, age or mental health

Here are some ways of opening a conversation for various situations:

For Prospects/ Customers:
- ✓ What were some of the key initiatives you took that brought you this far?
- ✓ What makes you stand out from your competitor?
- ✓ What's the most exciting thing about your business?
- ✓ What's the most exciting thing about your team?
- ✓ What are some of the most significant changes in your industry in recent years?
- ✓ If you could go back one year in time, what would you do differently?
- ✓ I'm honestly curious to know your story
- ✓ Tell me about your...?
- ✓ What's your company's biggest priority right now?
- ✓ How has business changed since we talked last?
- ✓ How are your efforts in [related business area]?
- ✓ What can I do to help you achieve….?

Common event
- ✓ What do you think of the conference so far? ... How have the sessions been? What did you particularly like?
- ✓ What inspired you to become a member of this body?

Company/Job
- ✓ Tom mentioned of how you were recently given   additional responsibilities…Congratulations!

- ✓ How do you like this new role? What are some of the new areas responsibilities now? How different is it to what you were doing?

Business/Industry
- ✓ Off what I know, you were all along into production? How and what made you get into this active sales role?
- ✓ How have the recent changes in the government regulations affecting your business?

Location
- ✓ I live in Delhi. Where are you from?
- ✓ This is my very first visit to Mauritius. What do you recommend I see while I'm here?
- ✓ What is it that you like about living in Colombo?

Sports
- ✓ I hear that your favorite past time is playing golf. Did you see the xxxx Cup this year?
- ✓ Last night's cricket match kept me in real suspense. What did you feel about it?

Travel
- ✓ Sarah was mentioning that you just returned from Turkey. How was your trip?
- ✓ I know you'd been to Israel recently. Our family is also planning a trip sometime next year. How do you recommend we go about this?

Hobbies/Interests
- ✓ I noticed that you volunteered in the company's cancer prevention drive? That's certainly a good deed to do. How did the event go?
- ✓ What are your hobbies or interests outside of work?

Some Common Conversation Killers
How do you know if a question is too personal? Ask yourself how you would feel if someone asked you the question and everybody in the room could hear the answer. If you'd feel comfortable, the question is OK.
Avoid:
- ✓ Bragging
- ✓ Interrupting
- ✓ Monopolizing
- ✓ Not playing the game

If someone asks a question, give him or her something to work with. Don't do this: "How was your vacation?' "Fine"

Instead: "How was your vacation?" "Fine The beach was great and we went boating every day."

With your Boss
When you are out with your boss for lunch or dinner...
Here are a few points you can keep in mind while on a dinner/lunch with your boss.
- ✓ Focus on your attire-Dress Professionally
- ✓ Be punctual and on time
- ✓ Be active and enthusiastic all the time
- ✓ Watch your body language and mannerisms
- ✓ Maintain a presence of mind and positive attitude
- ✓ Let your host take the lead
- ✓ Stay focused
- ✓ Pick appropriate topics- do some groundwork, know what to talk about
- ✓ Matchup to the audience at food and drinks
- ✓ Express your gratitude

Things to talk while having lunch or dinner with your boss:
- ✓ Sports
- ✓ Music
- ✓ Literature: depending on his/her age
- ✓ Office history: their years of experience, his/her climb up, his/her challenges
- ✓ Assignments/ Projects
- ✓ Food
- ✓ Hobbies

Few things which your boss may want to hear from you
- ✓ Things you enjoy doing
- ✓ Things you find boring
- ✓ About your knowledge gaps
- ✓ Feedback and goals
- ✓ New innovative methods to implement
- ✓ How your life has been influenced by the company
- ✓ Career progression

Things to avoid talking while having lunch with your boss:
- ✓ Don't get too personal:
- ✓ Strictly avoid prejudiced topics
- ✓ Do not blabber/ blurt out others mistakes
- ✓ Be careful about your remarks: Think of the repercussions before you speak
- ✓ Do not whine or complain
- ✓ Never talk office politics/ gossip
- ✓ Toilet humor
- ✓ Indiscretions: You cross your limit and lose the impression in front of the boss

Drinks and Wine Etiquette

Restaurants are happy to provide complimentary tastes of wine because they know that it will make you more comfortable ordering a glass. It's okay to ask for a taste of wines offered by the glass, since those wine bottles are already opened. However, if you plan to order a bottle from the wine list, you'll need to proceed without the benefit of a sample.

When the wine steward brings the bottle, check the label to be sure it is the exact wine that was ordered. Feel the cork after the wine is opened. Check for moistness, which is one way to determine whether or not the wine has been properly stored. A cork that is too dry or damaged will let air into the bottle and damage the wine. Smell the cork to make sure there is no unpleasant odor. A hint of vinegar will indicate the wine has gone bad. Most restaurants offer a smaller selection of wines by the glass. When ordering wine by the glass, you should be aware that you may be getting wine from a previously opened bottle. You may want to ask the server when the bottle was opened. If it has been opened for one or more days, you may want to make another selection.

The first taste is offered to the host/hostess, who will take a sip and indicate approval or disapproval. The host/hostess is served last, after all the guests have been served.

If the host and/or others at the table order a glass of wine, you may do so if you wish. Formal dinners can serve a different wine with each course, and you do not have to finish each glass.

How to Order Wine? If you are unsure what to order, look at the menu and ask the waiter for a recommendation. Start by selecting a wine in the category you are interested in and find a wine at the price point you are comfortable with. Show the sommelier/ steward your selection and ask for his opinion, but place your finger on the price, rather than the name.

A good rule of thumb to determine how many bottles to order is to start with a half bottle per person. If the group includes at least three people, you may try ordering a bottle of red and a bottle of white.

The order of the wine glasses begins with the one closest to you:

- ✓ Sherry (Soup course)
- ✓ White wine is usually served with poultry and fish)
- ✓ Red wine is with the Meat course and usually preferred for dark meats and red meats and sauces
- ✓ Water goblet

How do you hold the wine glasses?

If you are drinking white wine, hold the glass by the stem.

If it is red wine, hold the glass by the bottom of the goblet

The reasons are practical. White wine is served more chilled than red, so holding the glass by the stem helps it to remain chilled. Red wine is served warmer than white, therefore the heat of your hand around the goblet will not diminish the wine's bouquet.

Hold your drink in your left hand to keep your right hand dry and ready to shake hands.

It is perfectly fine to refrain from alcoholic drinks

Never turn your wine glass over to indicate you do not want to drink. Simply use your hand on the glass to show that you are not interested. Whether you drink or not is a personal choice and you are not bound to give long-winded excuses as a reply. So do not make it sound as if drinking alcohol is a crime. Simply thank the host for offering the drink and state your preference. S/he would be glad to get you the drink of your choice.

One glass of wine may be acceptable.

Toasting Etiquette

Toasting to love, friendship, health, wealth and happiness has been practiced by almost every culture from the beginning of recorded history. Traditionally, the host or hostess offers the first toast. Around a table with friends, however, a guest can propose the first toast (and often does), usually as a way to thank the host for bringing everyone together. At a wedding however, it is usually the best man that leads the toasting at a wedding reception.
Unless your toast has been designated as the key one of the evening, think of K.I.S.S.- Keep it Short and Sweet or you can also think of 3 B's- Begin Right, Be Brief and Be Seated. The key toast is a small speech of sorts, and it should be composed in writing and rehearsed by the speaker well in advance.
The host always toasts first. Gain the crowd's attention by standing and raising your glass; banging on a glass with a knife should be considered a measure of last resort. Gentle is better than hearty when it comes to clinking. You don't want to be remembered as the one who smashed the glass and bathed everyone around you in red wine.
Make sure that all glasses are filled before toasting, and ensure that everyone is involved. Nothing is more uncomfortable than standing up in front of a room full of friends or strangers to propose a toast while having your request largely ignored, with all of them busy in their own groups. Instead, enlist the help of your colleagues and friends by asking them to assist in quieting their respective groups when they see you stand with your glass raised. At formal

occasions the person toasting stands, along with the others toasting, while the person being toasted remains seated.

There are many occasions where a toast is appropriate like weddings, anniversaries, christenings, Christmas and New Year parties, birthdays, reunions, retirements or for the birth of a child. If you know the occasion, you should prepare your toast in advance. Write it down, keep it brief and practice until you feel confident. Be sure to speak slowly and loud enough for all guests to hear.

Hold the glass up towards the center of the table, raising it only to eye level, ensuring you have eye contact with the person across from you.

If it is an informal party such as an example of a Christmas night, the host might just say something like this, "Thank you for coming and I'm delighted we are all here on this cozy Christmas night, as we get ready to welcome the New Year ahead of us. Here's to a glorious 2023."

The guests respond by taking a sip of their drinks - but never emptying the glass. A person who doesn't drink alcohol should join in as well, toasting with a soft drink or even water.

The person being toasted does not drink to himself. The best bet here is to do nothing except look humble and appreciative. Then after everyone has toasted, the person being toasted to, rises and initiates a return toast by saying a simple thanks and taking a sip. He may also raise his own glass to propose a toast to the host, or anyone else he sees fit to honor. It is no small feat to pull off a successful event, and honoring your host with a toast is a nice way to show your gratitude. Say something like, "Thank you for including all of us in such a fun and festive Christmas party. You went out of your way to make this night so special and your hard work has certainly paid off. Here's to Jonathan, a lovely and gracious host."

When in an informal gathering with glasses are raised it can just be with shouts of "Cheers!", "To your health and joy!" or "To Cindy and Bob!" Including a few personal remarks, praise, or a relevant story or joke –can be a good idea, provided the same is clean and in line with the event or occasion. Ideally, a good toast is one that is centered around the occasion or gathering and using a concluding phrase such as "Here's to?" or "Cheers."

At private or small informal dinners, it is acceptable for everyone-the one toasting, and the one being toasted included to remain seated.

Never refuse to participate; you can always use an empty glass or non-alcoholic beverage. The glasses don't have to hold wine like the others; non-drinkers can toast with water, juice, or a soft drink.

Tea Etiquette

The general time for tea is four o'clock in the afternoon, with service running sometimes from two to five o'clock. For this reason they are called "afternoon tea" or simply "tea" and not to be called "high tea", as it's not the same thing.

These afternoon teas are social events that can happen when you have to entertain a visiting friend, celebrate a special occasion, a house warming party and a wonderful way to spend time with friends. It is far less formal today, but some simple rules of etiquette still apply.

The tea session is made up of three courses of food with a pot of tea in the following order:
1. The savory course with finger sandwiches
2. The scones course served with clotted cream and jam
3. Sweet cakes pastries

Tea equipment and flatware

The standard china tea set consists of:
1. A teapot,
2. A creamer for the milk,
3. A sugar bowl,
4. A pitcher of hot water (for those who prefer weak tea), and
5. A plate for lemon slices.

Depending on the number of guests, the teacups, saucers and spoons are placed on the right side, while the flatware (for serving cakes, pastries, bread etc), plates, knives and butter spreaders and tea napkins are placed on the left. If there are dishes with jam and cream where everyone takes a portion, then each dish should have its own serving spoon. Never use your own utensils to dip into the jam or cream dish.

However, when seated at a table in a private home or in a tea-room, there should be at each place setting the following:

- ✓ A knife or butter spreader on the right side of the plate
- ✓ A fork on the left side.
- ✓ A teaspoon may be placed on the saucer holding the cup or to the right of the knife.

Here are some important Do's and Don'ts as you begin:

- ✓ The dress code these days is "smart casual". Suits and fancy dresses are not necessary. However, it may differ depending on the venue, so always be sure to check before attending.
- ✓ It is required that the host assigns one guest to pour tea for everyone at the table.
- ✓ Never serve yourself first (if you're the host!) or overfill the teacups.
- ✓ The assigned pourer will pour tea into an empty tea cup. Use a tea strainer if needed and fill the teacups up to three quarters of the way.
- ✓ Never add milk before adding tea to a tea cup, as not every guest drinks tea with milk, and adding the tea first gives the drinker the option of adding milk or not. You want to make sure to leave room to allow your guests to add milk, lemon or sweetener to their tea if desired.
- ✓ When you sit down instantly drape the napkin on your lap with the crease facing towards you. This will save you from any unsightly

spills and show that you're well versed in the art of dining etiquette.

✓ Stir the tea with a teaspoon up and down (6 o'clock to 12 o'clock motion) gently and noiselessly by moving 2-3 times without touching the sides of the teacup. Then set the teaspoon on the saucer behind the cup, with the handle of the spoon pointing in the same direction as the handle of the cup in a four O'clock position similar to a clock.

✓ Never leave a spoon upright in the cup, or place the spoon on the saucer in front of the cup or let the spoon drop, after stirring the tea, with a clank onto the saucer.

✓ When holding the teacup, it is done by meeting your thumb and index finger in the handle and resting your middle finger under it.

✓ Never hook your finger through the handle or stick your pinky out. That's a common mistake as most assume it's being fancy. But, pinkies out is not acceptable. When holding the teacup keep the pinkie down!

✓ The saucer stays on the table. Don't hold it in your hands while enjoying tea. You only hold your saucer and tea cup together if you are standing or sitting with no table in front of you.

✓ Don't wrap your hands around the cup.

✓ Wait for the tea to cool. Whilst blowing on hot tea might seem like the practical thing to do, this is actually considered bad manners in the world of afternoon tea.

✓ You may begin to eat the savories and tea sandwiches first, followed by the scones and then the sweets. You can use your fingers too as after all, afternoon tea is all finger foods!

- ✓ Break the scone in half by hand and eat each half separately or enjoy by breaking off bite-sized chunks. Spread cream first then top with jam.
- ✓ Do not use cutlery or be tempted to eat the sweet course first.
- ✓ At the end of the tea, the napkin is not refolded but picked up by the center and placed loosely to the left of the plate with the open edge to the right.
- ✓ Enjoy Yourself! Most importantly whilst following the rules of etiquette is important don't let yourself get so focused on them that you forget to enjoy the experience!

Tipping Etiquette

Note: (*As this book is addressed to an international audience, the tipping amounts are very general just to provide an idea. It is important to do your groundwork before you travel anywhere*)

Tipping is very important, yet it can be super confusing, as there is no true standard for tipping. When, who and how much to tip can depend on any number of factors, including the specific situation, service, or even the location. Tipping however, is all about showing appreciation for good service. Standard tipping amounts on average usually range from 5% to 20%, with anything above 20% indicating excellent service, but this definitely does vary with the service provider, service received, culture and country

Here are some general guidelines:
- ✓ Tip on the pre-tax amount of the bill, not on the total.
- ✓ Do not make a show of the amount being tipped. It must be done discreetly.
- ✓ The usual tip internationally, is ten (10) to twenty (20) percent on the pre-tax amount of the bill
- ✓ Sometimes a gratuity is already included in the bill. But if you think it is deserved, you can leave an additional amount.
- ✓ Sometimes a restaurant may have a 'no-tipping' policy. In such cases, you may want to leave a note of appreciation, or ask to see a

manager and share what you loved most about the server
- ✓ Not every country has a culture of tipping- So keep in mind that tipping etiquette can change depending on country/ culture. If the service is bad, you don't have to tip, when you're not satisfied with the service.
- ✓ If the service is good, being generous can help with even better service in future.
- ✓ There is no need to tip the owner or proprietor of the restaurant, even if he or she serves you.
- ✓ You also do not need to tip the maitre d' unless they have done a special favor or arranged a special meal for you.

Here are some general Tipping Percentages
- ✓ Self-service restaurants/ Buffet: 5-10%
- ✓ Extra accommodating waiters: a few additional bucks for extra special service
- ✓ Waiter (serving at tables):15-20% pre-tax
- ✓ Lingering at your table on a busy night: an extra: 10 to 15%
- ✓ Waiter (buffet): 10%
- ✓ Bartender: 15-20%
- ✓ Host or Maitre d': Not necessary just for greeting you and showing you to your table. But a small amount for going above and beyond to find you a table on a busy night or on occasion, if you are a regular patron
- ✓ Tip for Delivery: 10-15% of the bill depending on the size of the order and difficulty of delivery
- ✓ Massage therapists: 15% to 20%,
- ✓ Hairdressers or nail technicians: 10% to 20%

- ✓ Restroom Attendant- depending on the level of service
- ✓ Valet: Tip when the car is returned to you.
- ✓ Uber driver: 15% to 20% of the fare for taxi services
- ✓ Musicians
- In some posh restaurants with piano/ musical instrument entertainment, you do not tip the musician unless there is tip jar.
- If you have made song requests, tip them and do so for each song.
- You needn't stop eating when musicians perform table side. Just smile and thank them as you tip when the musicians finish.

Settling the Bill

As a Guest:
If you are someone's guest at a meal, ask the person what he/she recommends. By doing this, you will learn price range guidelines and have an idea of what to order. Usually order an item in the mid price range. Also keep in mind, the person who typically initiates the meal will pay. The person who does the inviting does the paying. If someone invites you to lunch and the server places the bill on the table, don't make a grab for it if you are a guest. Let the person who invited you have the opportunity to pick up the bill and deal with it. If being treated by someone, always thank them

As the Host:
If you are the host, tell the maitre d' or waiter in advance that you should receive the bill. If the server gives the bill to your guest ask them for the bill. A simple way to prevent this from happening is to let the server or maitre d' know in advance that the bill should be brought to you. Discretely review the bill. Signal the waiter when you would like to pay by putting the bill holder to the edge of the table, with the bills or the credit card sticking out.
Tell the waiter if you would like them to keep the change. You should prearrange how the bill is being paid by you-cash, card, or other means. Remember to tip your waiter a good amount for moderate service; and a much bigger tip for excellent service.
If there is a problem with the bill, quietly discuss it with the waiter. If the waiter is not cooperative,

excuse yourself from the table and ask to speak to the manager.

If your Credit Card is declined:
Do not call attention to the situation
If your card continues to be declined, and you do not have enough cash to pay, ask to pay by cheque, or visit the nearest ATM, or send through someone or return the next day with cash.
If the restaurant declines these suggestions, you have no option but to return to the table and throw yourself at the mercy of your companions.
Repay their kindness within 24 hours, in cash.

Business Meal Follow-up:
Thank you notes

The Thank You Note

When to send one: A handwritten thank you note must be sent in response to:

- ✓ Gifts- any kind
- ✓ Dinner, parties or get-togethers
- ✓ After a meal outside/ or at their home
- ✓ Congratulations- on a milestone, an event or achievement, job/college interview
- ✓ Contributions made- sponsors of any of your events, fund raiser, etc.
- ✓ Any other time that is appropriate

Remember that it takes only a minute to write a quick note, but the reward is much greater than just a verbal "thank you" or phone call. A thank you note need not be lengthy- its purpose is only to convey gratefulness. Your note should be sent in a timely manner, however better late than never

What should Thank You Notes cover?

A note has two advantages: a) it doesn't interrupt the other person's time 2) it comes across as warmer and more gracious. This is why it is more preferred to a phone call.

It must ideally contain:

- ✓ A formal greeting and salutation
- ✓ A display of gratitude-Something unique, special or memorable about the event, gift or gesture
- ✓ Expressing to the guest how nice it was to dine with him/ her and briefly recapping any business details.

✓ Any details that show that you remember the party/ event and how you had a good time

How should the notes be?
✓ Notes should be sent promptly.
✓ Thank you notes are usually written on a small fold-over note (usually 3 x 5 or 4 x 6) or on a correspondence card (flat card, usually 4 x 6)
✓ If using the fold-over note, write on page 3. If using the correspondence card, write only on the front. Use Blue or Black Ink
✓ Begin with the Greeting: *Dearest Aunt,* Write your appreciation: *The grey sneakers is just amazing. It fits so snug-Appreciate a lot and thank you very much!* Mention its use: *I am sure going to use these to all my college parties.* Look ahead: *I'm looking forward to seeing you soon during the next set of holidays in September.* Close: *Love always, Cynthia*

Here's a sample:
Dear Sarah,
Thank you for that delicious dinner we had last night. I really appreciate all the trouble you put in, in going out of the way to make Jonathan and myself so at ease.
Most of all were those helpful and powerful inputs that you shared with us that will now enable us have a clearer understanding of the upcoming project that we are so excited to be working along with you. I know together, we will make this a resounding success!
Thank you once again.

Sincerely yours,
Gerard
Title
Company Name (logo)

Reciprocating to the Invitation

When you invite someone to a business lunch, dinner, or breakfast, it does not always mean they are obligated to reciprocate. This is particularly more appropriate to business situations where you are not expected to repay an invitation to a strictly-business meal, no matter who invited you - a customer, a client, or your boss. But you may certainly want to do so if you are looking at continuing business together. So also, it applies to a customer who has been entertained by a salesperson or supplier-is not expected to return the invitation, even if his or her spouse or family was invited.

However, for social settings, you will need to return social invitations from your colleagues, friends and other business associates.

Conclusion

Success may look different for everyone, but practicing good work etiquette, being professional, productive and respectful to people around you will help you achieve your ultimate goal. These skills will not only serve you well now, but also in the future. In today's competitive environment, carrying yourself professionally and managing yourself at the dinner table is an area of expertise that is much sought after.

The Golden Rule of Etiquette is that when you are in doubt; discretely watch until others show the way. Keep in mind that etiquette rules are not commandments- learn the standards and then apply them as you see fit.

When you become comfortable with what you've learned, most of this becomes second nature- completely natural to you. Remember, that knowing most of this information and being sincere, will give you the confidence to tackle all situations ahead of you, so you can concentrate on your business at hand!

And if you do forget some of this, you have one very important rule to remember and fall back on- Always use: Common sense, Respect, Compassion, and Kindness. Always take the higher ground, and do not respond to rudeness with rudeness.

Etiquette is after all, behaving yourself a little better than is absolutely essential... so I wish you well moving further up your career with Great Personal and Professional Success!

About the Author
'GERARD ASSEY'

Gerard Assey is a Graduate in Economics, a PGD in Management (HRD) and holds a Doctorate in Leadership. Gerard holds several International Qualifications in Sales, Debt Collection, Training & Teaching, and is a 'Fellow' of the prestigious 'Institute of Sales & Marketing Management'-UK, a Certified NLP Practitioner, a 'Certified Trainer', an 'Accredited Management Teacher-Behavioral Sciences', a 'Certified Competency Facilitator', a 'Certified Management Consultant'- (the International credentials of a professional management consultant, awarded in accordance with global standards of the ICMCI); and a Certification from the University of Michigan in 'Successful Negotiation: Essential Strategies and Skills'

He is also a Member of the 'National Association of Sales Professionals' backed with several years experience in varied industries, both in India and Overseas. He also holds an 'Etiquette Consultant' Certification from the USA (by Sue Fox, Author of Best Seller: 'Business Etiquette for Dummies'. She has trained some of the top celebrities' world over). He was also a recipient of a scholarship for extensive training in Japan on 'Corporate Management for India'.

Gerard Assey is 'Founder & Chief Corporate Trainer' of the Group: **'Citius, Altius, Fortius Unlimited'**- an organization that **celebrated 20 years of Glorious**

Service in 2021, focusing on 3 Core Competencies: **People. Performance. Profit**; in functional areas of Sales & Marketing, HR & Organizational Development, covering Recruitment, Training & Consultancy!

Having managed organizations with large Sales Forces in India & Overseas, his specialization cover extensive areas of Sales Training (All levels - Presentation, Negotiation, Key/ Strategic Accounts Management & Managerial Skills for all sectors), Bid Proposal/ Capture Planning/ Management Trainings, Retail Sales, Customer Service & Customer Retention Programs, Training for Prevention & Collection of Debt, Self & Personal Development Programs (Time Management, Teamwork & Team Building, Business Etiquette & Personal Grooming, Leadership & Managerial Skills, People Management Skills, Train-the-Trainer etc), including preparation of Custom-designed Business Manuals for Internal (HR, Induction, and Sales etc) & External use (Instruction, User Manuals).

Gerard has successfully conducted over 5900 Trainings & Workshops (as of Nov '22) all across India, Middle East, Africa, Europe & S.E. Asia. Besides public programs conducted regularly, both in India & Overseas, he has some of the top names as clients whom he services from Single Owners to large Public & Government undertakings, covering all sectors, for their in-house needs.

His website: www.CollectionSkills.com is the only one in this part of the world to be featured in the 'Collections & Credit Risk Magazine-USA' under 'Who's Who in Training' and ranks TOP, along with other websites listed below on most search engines.

Gerard is author of 47 books already (as on Nov 2022),
A few of the business related books being:
1. Bite-sized Bits on Commonsense Management
2. Heart to Heart on Life's Principles'
3. How to become a Successful Manager
4. The Sales Professionals' Master Workbook of S.Y.S.T.E.M.S
5. The Professional Business Email Etiquette Handbook & Guide
6. The Professional Business Video-Conferencing Etiquette Handbook & Guide
7. Professional Presentation Skills
8. Exceptional Customer Service
9. Professional Tele-Marketing Skills
10. Professional Debt Collection Skills
11. The G.R.E.A.T. Sales & Service Workbook
12. Sales Training Advantage for Results (*The Ultimate Sales Training Manual
to enable you stand out as a S.T.A.R.*)
13. CEO Daily Planner & Organizer
14. The Sales Professionals' Master Daily Planner
15. The Professional Debt Collector's Master Daily Planner
16. My Daily Planner & Organizer
17. MY EMERGENCY INFORMATION RECORD (Family Emergency & Peace of Mind Planner)
18. The Ultimate Therapist & Counselors Planner and Organizer
19. Building an Ethical Workplace
20. Managing Relationships at Work
21. Managing Business Meetings Effectively
22. Effective Delegation Skills
23. Goal Setting for Success
24. B2B Selling by Email
25. Professional Business Etiquette & Grooming

Besides regularly contributing to business & trade journals, including international ones such as the 'Creative Training Techniques' and the 'Sales News' of the U.S.A, He is also a member of several prestigious bodies & trade associations, having participated in many Conferences & Workshops in India & Overseas.

Prior to his last assignment of leading & managing a large MNC as head, Gerard had a 3-year stint in the Middle East as a Consultant with a leading British Consultancy Firm.

As the past 'Official Country Representative' for the International Business Award- 'THE STEVIES'-(the business world's own Oscar) for about 4 years- he ensured a few Indian companies that qualify for the same every year!

Gerard can be contacted at:

Email: training@Sales-Training.in,training@CollectionSkills.com

Websites:

www.Sales-Training.in
www.EtiquetteWorks.in
www.CollectionSkills.com
www.RetailSalesTraining.in
www.SalesTrainingIndia.com
www.ManualPreparation.com
www.TrainingWithPuppets.com
www.FirstContactAcademy.com
www.SalesAndMarketingRecruiter.com

Our TRAININGS & BOOKS that can help your team

- ✓ **Sales Effectiveness**: Selling Skills for any Sector: Service/ Logistics/ FMCG Realty/ Insurance & Finance/ Media/ SPA's, Health Clubs & Salons/ Key Account Management, Effective Negotiation Skills/ Bid & Proposal Management Skills/ Retail Sales Training: Any Sector (Auto, Jewelry, Clothing, Luxury etc)
- ✓ **Customer Service Skills**-Complaints Handling & Customer Retention
- ✓ **Debt Prevention & Collection Skills**
- ✓ **Etiquette & Grooming**
- ✓ **Leadership & Managerial Skills**
- ✓ **Self & Personal Development Skills**: Presentation Skills/ Effective Communication Skills/Business Proposal Writing Skills/ Problem Solving & Decision Making Skills/ Empowering Secretaries-The perfect PA! (For Secretaries & PA's)/ Effective Time Management/ Teamwork & Teambuilding/ P.R.I.D.E- **P**ersonal **R**esponsibility **I**n **D**elivering **E**xcellence

A Few of Our Business Books
By the Top Corporate Trainer & Author of 47 Books! (Nov '22)
And...DAILY PLANNERS for Every Corporate Need!
Available Online on all leading Stores